THE GREAT WHITE HOPE

is the remarkable new play about the tumultuous career of the first black heavyweight champion of the world—his savage drive, unabashed defiance in the face of crushing prejudice, and his flaunted, and finally tragic, affair with a white girl.

" . . . THE MOST SIGNIFICANT DRAMA OF THE DECADE. TOPICAL AS THE MOST ADVANCED PRODUCTS OF THE AVANT GARDE."

—Baltimore Sun

". . . A TUMULTUOUS, IRRESISTIBLE AVALANCHE OF A PLAY, which hurls itself from the stage. There were moments on opening night when I wondered if the only way to keep from being knocked unconscious by it would be to crawl under my seat at the Alvin."

—The New Yorker

BROADWAY'S NEWEST

"A SPRAWLING, BOISTEROUS LARGER-THAN-LIFE PLAY. A VIRILE AND EN-GROSSING DRAMA."

—Jack Gaver, **United Press International**

"AN EXCITING NEW DRAMA, sometimes touching, sometimes brutal, occasionally deeply moving, always theatrical in the best sense of the term."

—**Chicago Daily News**

"TREMENDOUS! ONE OF THE GREAT THEATRE EXPERIENCES OF MY LIFE."

—Ed Sullivan

"A FASCINATING, OVERWHELMING HIT!"

—Leonard Lyons

"THE GREAT WHITE HOPE IS AN EX-TRAORDINARY NEW PLAY. This work is completely open, within the reach of the largest or the smallest audience; it is dramatically and artistically powerful and moving."

—**The New York Review of Books**

THE GREAT WHITE HOPE

a play by
Howard Sackler

A NATIONAL GENERAL COMPANY

THE GREAT WHITE HOPE

*A Bantam Book / published by arrangement with
The Dial Press, Inc.*

PRINTING HISTORY
Dial edition published 1968
Bantam edition published April 1969
2nd printing
3rd printing
4th printing
5th printing

*Bantam Books are published by Bantam Books, Inc., a subsidiary
of Grosset & Dunlap, Inc. Its trade-mark, consisting of the words
"Bantam Books" and the portrayal of a bantam, is registered in the
United States Patent Office and in other countries. Marca Registrada.
Bantam Books, Inc., 271 Madison Avenue, New York, N.Y. 10016.*

ACKNOWLEDGMENTS

"Grizzly Bear" (p. 141†) / Words by Irving Berlin / Music by George Botsford. © Copyright 1910 Irving Berlin, 1650 Broadway, New York, N.Y. © Copyright renewed 1937 Irving Berlin and Mills Music, Inc., N.Y. Reprinted by permission of Irving Berlin Music Corporation, New York, N.Y. and Mills Music, Inc., New York, N.Y.

"I Always Think I'm Up in Heaven (When I'm Down in Dixieland)" (p. 162*) / Words by Sam M. Lewis and Joe Young / Music by Maurice Abrahams. Copyright © 1919 by Waterson, Berlin & Snyder Co., Inc. Copyright assigned to Mills Music, Inc. 1932. Copyright renewed (USA) 1946 by Mills Music, Inc., Robbins Music Corp., and Warock Corp. World rights outside USA controlled by Mills Music, Inc. Used by permission.

for Regina Vasquez Bello

who shortly after sunrise on several mornings in 1915
watched from a window of her father's ranch-house
outside Havana and saw the World's Heavyweight
Champion, jogging along the road; once or twice they
waved to each other, and she spoke of it to me nearly
50 years later.

ACT 1

ACT 2

ACT 3

TIME: the years preceding the First World War

Cast of Characters

FRANK BRADY, *the retired champion*
FRED, *his manager*
CAP'N DAN, *a champion of earlier days*
SMITTY, *a famous sportswriter*
GOLDIE, *Jack's manager*
JACK JEFFERSON
TICK, *his trainer*
ELLIE BACHMAN, *Jack's girl*
CLARA, *Jack's former girlfriend*
BLACKFACE, *an entertainer*
COLONEL COX
DEACON
DONNELLY, *Mrs. Bachman's attorney*
MRS. BACHMAN, *Ellie's mother*
CAMERON, *Chicago District Attorney*
DIXON, *a Federal agent*
SCIPIO, *a street philosopher*
MRS. JEFFERSON, *Jack's mother*
PASTOR
RUDY, *a baseball player*
TREACHER, *Jack's solicitor*
EUBANKS, *his aide*
SIR WILLIAM GRISWOLD, *Home Office Undersecretary*
COATES, *Chairman of British Vigilance Board*
MRS. KIMBALL, *a landlady*
INSPECTOR WAINWRIGHT, *Metropolitan Police*
BRATBY, *Olympic Sporting Club officer*
FARLOW, *London County Council*
KLOSSOWSKI, *a Polish heavyweight*
POP WEAVER, *a promoter*
RAGOSY, *a Hungarian impresario*
NEGRO, *an African student*
PACO, *a Mexican boy*
EL JEFE, *a Mexican politico*
A Young Federal AGENT
THE KID

Reporters, photographers, trainers, handlers, fight fans, gamblers, Nevada Rangers, weigher-in, barker, Temperance marchers, civic leaders, musicians, revelers and mourners, brothers and sisters of the congregation, French crowd, German officers, Hungarian audience, stagehands, Pinkerton men, Cuban boys.

THE GREAT WHITE HOPE

ACT 1

scene one

Brady's farm, in Parchmont, Ohio.

Enter BRADY, *the heavyweight champion;* FRED, *his manager;* CAP'N DAN, *a champion of earlier days;* SMITTY, *a famous sportswriter; several other* PRESS-MEN *and* PHOTOGRAPHERS; *a few* TRAINERS. GOLDIE, *Jack Jefferson's manager, in the background.*

BRADY

Get Burke, or Kid Foster. Big Bill Brain!
I ain't gonna fight no dinge.

FRED
Now, Frank—

CAP'N DAN
Listen here to me, Franklin—

BRADY
You wouldn't fight one when you had the belt!

CAP'N DAN
Well, let's say none of them came up to it then.
It wasn't that I wouldn't, I didn't have to.

FRED
He didn't have to, Frank, but you do.

BRADY
In your hat I do! I know what retired means,

1

and that's what I am. All I have to do
is dip the sheep and pay taxes.

CAP'N DAN

Hear that, boys? It's old Farmer Brown!

FRED

Sure looks retired, don't he! Look at the arms on him.

PRESSMAN 1

Three months back on the mill, that's all you need—

SMITTY

How long is it you put away Stankiewiez—

FRED

Not even a year! And if you smoked him in seven—

TRAINER 1

You'll get this one in five—

PRESSMAN 2
Four!

FRED
Two!
They got glass jaws, right, Cap'n Dan?

BRADY

I ain't gonna fight no dinge.

CAP'N DAN
Now, Franklin,
when you retired with that gold belt last summer,
nobody thought it would work out like this.
Everybody just thought that Sweeney'd fight Woods,
and whoever won that would be the new Number One,
    right?
So when the nigger asked could he fight Woods first
we figured, what the hell, it'll keep up the interest—

nobody, least of all Woods, thought he would lick him.
And then when he said he wants to try out Sweeney too,
why Sweeney never puts the gloves on with a nigger,
everybody knew that—besides, he was in Australia.
Nobody thought the nigger would go all that way to him,
and even when he did, who would have thought
he could needle old Tommy into taking him on?

SMITTY

I was down in Melbourne for the paper, Mr. Brady,
and let me tell you,
no paper here could print how bad it really was.
He'd say, Hit me now, Tommy, and then he'd let him,
grinning all the time, and then cuffing him, jabbing him,
making smart-ass remarks to the crowd—wouldn't
be a man and just knock him out, no,
and then, when they stopped it,
with Tommy there bleeding,
he's still got that big banjo smile on him—Jesus.

PRESSMAN 1

You're the White Hope, Mr. Brady!

BRADY

I'm the what?

PRESSMAN 2
The White Hope!
Every paper in the country is calling you that.

FRED

Frank, he lands in San Francisco tomorrow—come on!

BRADY (*to* CAP'N DAN)
Honest, I don't like this any more than you do.

CAP'N DAN

How're you going to like it
when he claims the belt's his because you won't fight him.

The heavyweight belt, son, yours and mine,
he can say it's his.

SMITTY

Just grin and put it on.

CAP'N DAN

How're you going to like it when the whole damn
    country
says Brady let us down, he wouldn't stick a fist out
to teach a loudmouth nigger, stayed home and let him
be Champion of the World.

SMITTY

Don't do it, Mr. Brady.

BRADY

I'll tell you the truth, Cap'n Dan. I hate to say it,
but I feel too old. I mean it, that's the truth.

FRED

The doc says different and I do too—

TRAINER 1

He's thinkin old because he's worried what to do—

BRADY

Shut up. Cap'n Dan, you know what I mean.

CAP'N DAN

I know you trust me and I say you're up to it—
and, Franklin, God Almighty hates a quitter!
Listen here, I'll confess something to you,
I had this lots of times when I was your age,
every time I had a fight or a birthday.

BRADY

How'd you get rid of it?

CAP'N DAN

The one way there is:
plenty of heat and nice deep massage.
Now, Frank, go inside. Mrs. Brady wants to show you
a letter I brought for you. I paid a call in Washington
on my way out here, and even though I think
it'll make you so big-headed you won't be fit to talk to,
you read it, then come out here and we'll see where we
stand.

(*Exit* BRADY. GOLDIE *comes forward*)

GOLDIE

Good, so it's fixed?

CAP'N DAN

Somebody say something?

GOLDIE

Me. I'm asking, Is it settled please, gentlemen?
You tell me Yes I can maybe catch the train.

CAP'N DAN

The man's in a hurry, Fred.

FRED

What about terms?

GOLDIE

What, you expect I'm gonna yell about terms?
Look, we're no babies here, you know like I know,
my Jackie would fight it for a nickel, tomorrow.
But it wouldn't look nice for you to take advantage,
so you'll offer me low as you can get away with
and I'll say OK.

FRED

Eighty-twenty, Goldie.

GOLDIE

What! A world's championship? You can't go twenty-five?

FRED

Eighty-twenty. That's it.

GOLDIE

Well . . . God bless America.

FRED

And Cap'n Dan to be the referee.

GOLDIE

Fred, you're kidding me?

FRED

Him or forget it. You know how it works.

GOLDIE

I don't mean no disrespect, but—

CAP'N DAN

Who'd you have in mind, friend, Booker T. Washington?

GOLDIE

All right, all right. Boy! What else?

FRED

That's all.

GOLDIE

He don't have to fight with his feet tied together?

FRED

I said that's all.

CAP'N DAN

We better set the place.

GOLDIE

Any place, name it, the Coast, Chicago—

CAP'N DAN

No big towns, Fred. You'll have every nigger
and his brother jamming in there.

GOLDIE

For my money
they could have it in Iceland!

SMITTY

How about Tulsa?
Denver? Reno?

PHOTOGRAPHER 1

Hey, Reno, that's OK!

PRESSMAN 1

Small.

FRED

No—wait—

TRAINER 2

Reno—

CAP'N DAN

Why not? The good old Rockies.

FRED

Yeah—

CAP'N DAN

A white man's country!

GOLDIE

Sure, but you can find them?

FRED

They'll come from all over, it's on the main line now—

SMITTY
And it's high and dry. Mr. Brady would like that—

TRAINER 2
The drier the better!
If that nigger gets a sweat up, one good whiff
and Frank'll be finished.

(*Enter* BRADY *carrying the gold belt*)

BRADY
Well, he's not through yet!

CAP'N DAN
There we are—

BRADY
Want some photos, boys?

PHOTOGRAPHER 1
Sure thing, Mr. Brady—

PHOTOGRAPHER 2
With it on, OK?

(PHOTOGRAPHERS *set up cameras.* PRESSMEN *ready notebooks*)

GOLDIE
A deal?

FRED
It's a deal.

(FRED *and* GOLDIE *shake hands*)

BRADY
And it's gonna be a pleasure—
tell your nigger I said so!

PRESSMAN 1
Pour it on, Mr. Brady—

GOLDIE
I should miss a train for this?

BRADY   (*rolling up his sleeves*)
You tell Mr. Black Boy to give me that smile
when he's inside those ropes—

TRAINER 1   (*to* PRESSMEN)
Get it down, get it down—

BRADY
I'll appreciate it, tell him—
my eyes ain't too good these days, you understand,
I like something nice and shiny to aim at—

(*Puts on belt*)

OK, boys?

PRESSMAN 1
Ah!

PHOTOGRAPHER 2
Stance, please, Mr. Brady—

(BRADY *takes stance;* PHOTOGRAPHERS' *magnesium
flares till end of scene*)

FRED   (*leading* GOLDIE *off*)
Don't let your boy take this nigger stuff to heart, huh?
Explain how it's going to pack em in, that's all.

GOLDIE
He knows how it is. Good luck!

(*Exits*)

FRED (*calling after him*)
You're OK, Goldie!

SMITTY (*to* CAP'N DAN, *looking
at* BRADY)
Well, there we are!

CAP'N DAN
Oh, he's the man all right.
I just don't like the idea of calling it a Hope,
I wish you boys hadn't hung that tag on him.

SMITTY
It's sure caught on, though!

CAP'N DAN
That's what bothers me, I guess.

SMITTY
Can I quote you on that?

CAP'N DAN
No, lend me a comb.
I better go stand up with him and get my picture took!

(*Laughter and* BLACKOUT. *Thudding of a punching-
bag, then* LIGHTS UP *on—*)

scene two

a small gym, San Francisco.

JACK JEFFERSON *shadow-boxing.* TICK, *his Negro
trainer.* ELEANOR BACHMAN, *a white girl, watching.*

TICK

Mix it up, Jack honey, pace him, pace him out,
hands up higher now, move, he's jabbin—
don't follow them head fakes, you watch his body,
there you go, jab! jab! Beauty—
fake with the body, not just the head, baby—
feint! jab! hook in behind it—
send him the right now—no! Whut you at?

JACK (*continuing his
movements*)

Givin him a right—

TICK
An where you givin it?

JACK

Chin bone—

TICK
Sucker bone! Boy, you a worry!
He groggy now, right, you jabbin his liver
till he runnin outa gas an his eyes goin fishy—
Why you knock on dat chin! Could be ya done whut!

JACK

Wake him up, wake him up—

TICK

Watch him! He's bobbin, he's comin to you, block it—
where you gonna take dat right now?

JACK
Temple—

TICK

How!

JACK
Hook it, hook to de temple—

TICK

Why!

JACK

Softes place on his head—

TICK

Yeah! now you listenin to me, sugar!
Hook him again, a beauty, three now—

(JACK *stops*)

Hey, whut you doin—

JACK (*to* ELEANOR)

Now, honey, you juss know you tired a sittin here,
whyn't you go buy yourself a pretty or somethin—

ELLIE

No, let me stay. Unless you mind me here, Jack.

JACK

You mah Lady Luck! I don' mine you nowhere—

TICK

Oh, long as you lookin at him, he don' mine—

JACK

But ain't this too much rough-house for ya, honey?

ELLIE

Well—I try not to listen.

TICK

Much obliged!

ELLIE

Oh, Tick, I'm sorry—

JACK

She somethin, ain't she!

TICK
Darlin, you keep sittin there any way you like it,
cause he sure workin happy. OK?

ELLIE
OK!

TICK (*to* JACK)
Now, we gonna mooch or we gonna move?

JACK (*moves*)
Hole me dat bag! Gonna buss it wide open,
then we all go out an have a champagne lunch!

(*Enter* GOLDIE)

GOLDIE
Four soft-boiled eggs, that's what you're gonna have—

(*He does not notice* ELLIE)

JACK
Hey, Goldie!

TICK
How you doin, boss—

GOLDIE
Oy, those stairs—

JACK
Get him a chair, Tick—

GOLDIE
Cover him up first he shouldn't get ice on him.

JACK
Figured you stayin in Reno till tomorrow—

GOLDIE
What, we got it settled there—how do you feel?

TICK   (*puts robe on* JACK)
He feel like he look, boss!

GOLDIE
Not eating too quick?

TICK
No, sir, chewin good!

JACK
Ah's chewin till it hurts—

GOLDIE
Laugh, laugh!
This one you have to watch like a hawkeye!

JACK
Come on, Goldie, when it gonna be?

GOLDIE
The Fourth of July. Now the newspaper guys—

JACK (*laughing*)
The Fourth of July?

GOLDIE
So, it makes a difference?

JACK
No, it juss tickle mah funny-bone, dassall—

TICK
Fourth a July an Lawd you knows why!

GOLDIE
We should worry, listen, will we have a gate there—
fifteen thousand! Jack, you know what they're callin it?

Already by them it's the Fight of the Century—
twenty years I never seen such a hoopla!
Trains from St. Louis and Chicago, direct yet,
tents they have to put up, it's a regular madhouse,
and wait, from the ring they're gonna telegraph it, Jack,
straight to every Western Union in the country,
so like right away everybody should know,
and on that we make somethin too!

TICK

Lively times, Ah kin hear you comin!
Boy, you bout to win de Fight of de Century!

JACK

Yeah, or else lose an be the nigger of the minute.

GOLDIE (*noticing* ELLIE)

Listen, come here, Jack—

JACK
Whut kina odds goin?

GOLDIE

Brady eight to five. What's the girl doin here?

JACK

Oh, she looking roun. She don't bother us none.

GOLDIE

Lookin around for what?

JACK

You be nice now, Goldie—come on over, Ellie,
don't be shy now, hon—she a friend of mine, you know?

GOLDIE

Jackie, you gotta bring a girl here when you train?

JACK

Ah guess so, boss!
Ah loves to dance an prance fo de wimmins!

ELLIE

How do you do.

JACK
        Goldie, shake hands
with Miss Ellie Bachman.

GOLDIE
                Pleased to meetcha, Miss Bachman.
I apologize I didn't notice you before,
such a tumult we got here.

ELLIE
        Oh, sure, I understand.

GOLDIE

You're a fan of Jack's, huh?

JACK

Ellie was on the same boat from Australia,
she was visitin down there.

GOLDIE

Well, it's great to be home again, I bet.
You can't beat Frisco!

ELLIE
        Yes, I like it fine.
My home is in Tacoma, though.

GOLDIE
                Oh . . . it's awful damp up there,
    ain't it?

JACK

Mm-hmm! You know it!

ELLIE
        Yes, I can't say I miss it much.

    (Pause)

TICK

Uncle of mine work up dere in a laundry once,
he din like it neither . . .

JACK

Drizzle on you all the time there!

TICK

Right!

GOLDIE

Yeah, well, Miss Bachman,
the guys from the papers are comin any minute,
you know what I mean, so if maybe you excuse us—

JACK

She stay where she is.

TICK

Uh-oh.

GOLDIE

Jackie, look, what's the matter with you!

JACK

She stayin where she is.

GOLDIE

I'm gonna pass out here!

ELLIE

I'll wait in the room, Jack.

GOLDIE

In the room! Jesus Christ!

JACK

You be nice now, hear?

GOLDIE

I knew it!

Last night in my head it's like a voice—
Dumbbell, go home quick, somethin's goin on with him!

JACK

Ain't nobody's business!

GOLDIE

Grow up, for God's sake—

ELLIE

Let me go, it doesn't matter—

GOLDIE

No—please, one second—Tick, go lock the door.

(TICK *does*)

(*To* JACK)

So you don't know the score, huh?
Well, I'll tell you the score, right now I'll tell you.
And you should listen too, miss,
I can see you're a fine serious girl, not a bum,
better you should know, so there's no hard feelins here.
First, Jack, they hate your guts a little bit—OK!
You don't put on gloves everybody should like you.
Then they hate your guts some more—still OK!
That makes you wanna fight, some kinda pep it give you.
And then they hate you so much they're payin through
    the nose
to see a white boy maybe knock you on your can—
well, that's more than OK, cash in, after all,
it's so nice to be colored you shouldn't have a bonus?
But, sonny, when they start in to hate you more than
    that,
you gotta watch out. And that means now—
Oh, I got ears, I get told things—
guys who want to put dope into your food there,
a guy who wants to watch the fight behind a rifle.
OK, cops we'll get, dogs, that we can handle.

But this on top of it, a white girl, Jack,
what, do I have to spell it on the wall for you,
you wanna drive them crazy, you don't hear what happens—

 JACK

Whut Ah s'pose to do!
Stash her in a iddy biddy hole someplace in niggertown
an go sneakin over there twelve o'clock at night,
carry her roun with me inside a box
like a pet bunny-rabbit or somethin—

ELLIE
                              Jack—

JACK

Or maybe she juss put black on her face,
an puff her mouth up, so's nobody notice
Ah took nothin from em—

  (*Knock at door*)

                    Let 'em wait!
You know Ah done fool roun plenny, Goldie,
she know it too, she know it all,
but Ah ain't foolin roun now, unnerstand—

  (*Points to* TICK)

an if he say, "Thass whut you said lass time,"
Ah bust his nappy head—

                    TICK
                    I ain't sayin nothin!

  (*More knocking*)

                    GOLDIE
Hold on, I'm comin—

Jack, I swear, I'll help you,
just you shouldn't throw it in their face, Jack,
I'm beggin you—

JACK

See? This whut you fell inta, darlin.

ELLIE

Do what he says.

JACK

You go along with him?

ELLIE

Along with you, any way I can.

(*More knocking*)

GOLDIE

Go, sit over there—let em in, for Chrissake—

(TICK *admits* SMITTY *and several other* PRESSMEN)

TICK

Mornin, gents—

JACK

Hiya, fellers—Hey there, Smitty—

(*Handshaking and greeting*)

GOLDIE

Just a few minutes, fellers, OK?

PRESSMAN 1

Well, you're sure looking good, Jack.

JACK

Thanks, boss!

PRESSMAN 2
Guess you know about the Fourth—

PRESSMAN 1
You starting to get jumpy?

JACK
Yeah, Ah scared Brady gonna change his mind!

SMITTY
Still think you can take him, Jack?

JACK
Well, Ah ain't sayin Ah kin take him straight off—
an, anyway, dat be kina mean, you know,
alla dem people, big holiday fight—
how dey gonna feel Ah send em home early?

SMITTY
So your only worry is deciding which round.

JACK
Yeah, an dat take some thinkin, man!
If Ah lets it go too long in dere,
juss sorta blockin an keepin him offa me,
then evvybody say, "Now ain't dat one shif'less nigger,
why dey always so lazy?" An if Ah chop him down quick,
third or fourth roun, all at once then dey holler,
"No, t'ain't fair,
dat po' man up dere fightin a gorilla!"
But Ah gonna work it out.

PRESSMAN 2
What about that yellow streak Brady talks about?

JACK (undoing his robe)
Yeah, you wanna see it?

GOLDIE
Don't clown aroun, Jackie—

PRESSMAN 3

Any idea, Jack, why you smile when you're fighting?

JACK

Well, you know, Ah am a happy person.
Ah always feel good, huh? An when Ah'm fightin
Ah feels double good. So whut Ah wanna
put a face on for? An you know,
it's a sport, right, like a game,
so Ah like whoever Ah'm hittin to see
Ah'm still his friend.

PRESSMAN 2

Going to train in Chicago, Mr. Jefferson?

JACK

Yeah, Ah wanna see my little ole momma—

PRESSMAN 1

Fried chicken, Jack?

JACK
Mmm-mmh! Can't wait!

SMITTY

I believe that's Miss Bachman there, isn't it, Jack?
You first met on the boat?

ELLIE
No, not exactly—

GOLDIE

Miss Bachman is my secretary, we hired her in Australia,
she's from here, but she was over there and we, you know,
we hired her and she came over with the boys.

SMITTY

I see—

TICK

Boss, if dey finish Ah wanna rub him down—

PRESSMAN 1

We got plenty for now, Jack—

PRESSMAN 3

Thanks—

JACK

Come again!

PRESSMAN 2

Jack, one more question?

JACK

Yeah, go head.

PRESSMAN 2

You're the first black man in the history of the ring
to get a crack at the heavyweight title.
Now the white folks, of course, are behind the White
   Hope,
Brady's the redeemer of the race, and so on.
But you, Jack Jefferson, are you the Black Hope?

JACK

Well, Ah'm black and Ah'm hopin.

SMITTY

Try and answer him straight, Jack.

JACK

Oh, Ah guess mah cousins mostly want me to win.

SMITTY

You imply that some don't?

JACK

Maybe some a them reckon
they gonna pay a little high for that belt, if Ah take it.

SMITTY

Won't you try and change their minds, Jack,
get them all behind you?

JACK

Man, Ah ain't runnin for Congress!
Ah ain't fightin for no race, ain't redeemin nobody!
My momma tole me Mr. Lincoln done that—
ain't that why you shot him?

(*General laughter.* CLARA, *a Negro woman, bursts in*)

CLARA

My, oh my!
It de big black rooster and de little red hen!
I got you, you mother!

JACK

What you want here!

CLARA

I show you what I wants—

(*Goes for* ELLIE)

ELLIE

Jack!

JACK

Hey!

TICK (*restrains* CLARA)

You crazy, you bitch—?

GOLDIE

A little family quarrel, fellers,
see you tomorrow, you know how it is—

(THEY *remain*)

CLARA

You leave my man be, girl, you don' leave him,
Ah gonna throw you at him in chunks—

GOLDIE

You got it all wrong, Clara—

CLARA
                    Yeah? Ah gots it
from de chambermaid at the Park Royal Hotel,
Ah come all de way from Chicago to got it—

JACK

Now you got it you git you black ass outa here.

CLARA

Don' hit me!

JACK

Whut you tyin on, you evil chinch, you!

GOLDIE

Jack—fellers—

CLARA
            Sing it, daddy!
Let de gennumuns hear
how you smirchin your wife—

GOLDIE

What do you mean?

JACK
            She ain't no wife of mine—

CLARA

No which of what?
We's common law and Ah's comin home to poppa!

JACK

Ah's common nothin! Don' you poppa me, girl,
or Ah poppa you so you never forget it!
Ah quit on you when you cleared out a De-troit
wid Willie de pimp—

GOLDIE

Fellers, please, have a heart—Jack—

CLARA

Ah know you come after me, Ah know you was lookin—

JACK

You lucky Ah too busy to fine you, girl,
selling off mah clothes, mah ring, silver brushes—

CLARA

Gimme nother chance, baby, Ah misses you awful—

JACK

Don' come on with me! You juss smelling bread,
you comin here now cause you Willie's in jail—

CLARA

How you know where he at!

JACK

Ah from de jungle like you is, baby,
Ah hears de drums—

(*To* TICK)

                    take her over to Goldie's,
give her a twenty an carfare back.

TICK

                    Come on, Clara.

JACK

Ah tellin you once more, go way and stay there.

CLARA

You ain't closin up the book so easy, daddy—

(*To* ELLIE)

hear me, Gray Meat? Get it while you can!

TICK

Come on, out—

(*Drags her out*)

JACK (*to* ELLIE)
You all right, honey?

GOLDIE

Fellers, now I'm askin you, man to man, please,
for everybody's good, don't write nothin about it,
if it gets out, God knows what can happen—
I mean, look,
we wanna have a fight, don't we? And besides
the girl has a family, what the hell—

(*Pause*)

PRESSMAN 3

OK.

PRESSMAN 1
Don't worry, Goldie.

GOLDIE
Thanks, fellers, thanks—
let's all have a drink—

(*Hustles* THEM *out;* JACK *has begun punching the bag*)

ELLIE

Oh, Jack! It gets awful, doesn't it.

JACK
Well . . .
seems to get worse and better both at once.

ELLIE
Is there anything I can do?

JACK
Yeah . . .
Stick around. An don' never call me daddy.

(BLACKOUT—*sound of fireworks and band music*—
LIGHTS UP *on*—)

scene three

outside the arena, Reno.

Across the stage a banner: RENO THE HUB OF THE UNI-
VERSE. *Many small American flags in evidence. Stage
milling with* WHITE MEN *of every sort: at the center
a huge crap-game, at the rear a* BLACKFACE *performer
entertaining another* GROUP, *at one side a few* MEN
breaking up a fight, at the other a MAN *supporting a
singing* DRUNK, *in the foreground a* BETTOR *with a
fistful of money looking for a* TOUT.

ROLLER
Ooh, six, get ready, baby from Baltimore—

PLAYER 1
Shoot em—

TOUT (*to* BETTOR)
Sure, how much you bettin—

PLAYER 2

Boxcars!

PLAYER 1

Let it ride—

BETTOR

Ninety simoleons—

TOUT

Ninety on Brady at eight to five—

BETTOR

Eight—?

ROLLER

In or out—

BETTOR

Up yours eight, mister, they're giving eleven,
they're givin thirteen—

ROLLER

Who's in, who's in, who's—

BLACKFACE *(bursting in on*
the crap game)

Yassuh, yassuh, yassuh—

PLAYER 1

Hey, look who's here—

BLACKFACE

Move ovah, bredren, ole Doctuh Wishbone
gwine ta roll dem cubicles—
Uh oh! **Lonesome pockets!**
Kin ah come in wiv a chicken laig, boss?

(Flourishes one. Laughter)

PLAYER 3

Where's the white meat, Wishbone—

BLACKFACE

White meat? Oh, he puttin on de belt now—
an dark meat, he shakin in de graby!

(*Laughter, jeers.* THEY *all gather round*)

Lawd, Ah sho hopes dey's mo cullud folks den me
here—

ROLLER

Why's that, Wishbone—

BLACKFACE

Ah cain't bury all dat nigger bah mahself!

(*Laughter*)

Gwine ta read de sermon ovuh him, dassall—

BETTOR

Let's hear it!

BLACKFACE

"Bredren," it start, "kinely pass de plate"—no dat ain
it—

(*Laughter*)

"Bredren," it start, "come outer dem bushes"—no, tain't
dat neether—

(*Laughter*)

"Bredren"—here de one—"de tex for dis po' darkie
am foun in de Book ob"—well it roun bout de place
where Paul git off de steamboat. "Bredren," it say,
"bressed am dey dat lays down, **cause if dey ain gittin up
dey mought jes's well stays down"**—

(*Laughter, cheers,* SOMEONE *throws him a tambourine,* HE *sings*)

Ole Marse Brady whip cullud Jack
Come fum way down Souf,
Hair curl on his haid so tight
He coulden shet his mouf—

(THEY *all join in*)

Coon, coon, coon, ah wish mah culluh'd fade,
Coon, coon, coon, Lawd, make me a brahter shade—

(*Enter* COLONEL COX *with some* NEVADA RANGERS)

COX

All right, all right, stay where you are—

PLAYER 1

What the hell, Colonel—

PLAYER 2

Just having some fun—

COX

Boys, I got orders to confiscate all firearms—

(*Protests*)

We'll give em back tonight, after it's over—

RANGER 1 (*collecting weapons*)

Let's go—

RANGER 2

Thank you!

RANGER 1

Say, that's a real old one—

PLAYER 1 (*as band strikes
up nearby*)
What you fraid of, Colonel, we won't have to shoot him!

BETTOR
They're comin for the weigh-in!

(*Cheering nearby*)

COX (*to* BLACKFACE)
You'd better scram, Mike.

BLACKFACE
Sure thing, Colonel—

(*Runs off; more cheering; a scale is wheeled on*)

PLAYER 1 (*looks offstage*)
That's Brady's bus—here he comes—

(MUSIC *changes to "Oh, You Beautiful Doll"*)

ROLLER
Whack that nigger, Frank—

PLAYER 2
You fix him for us—

PLAYER 1
Wipe that smile off him, boy—

(THEY *all cheer as* BRADY, *in a robe and with his
hands taped, scowling, enters with* CAP'N DAN, FRED,
and entourage: HANDLERS, PRESS, *etc.* HE *gets on the
scale. Music stops*)

BRADY
Come on, it's hot as hell here. Let's go.

PRESSMAN 1

What did you have for lunch, Mr. Brady?

(*Laughter*)

BRADY

Nothin! A cuppa tea!

FRED

We'll get a statement in a minute, boys—

CAP'N DAN

Take it easy, Franklin—

WEIGHER-IN

Two hundred and four.

(*Cheers.* HE *steps off the scale, takes out a paper. Silence*)

BRADY

When I put on the gloves now and defend this here belt
it's the request of the public, which forced me out of
  retirement.
But I wanta assure them I'm fit to do my best,
and I don't think I'm gonna disappoint nobody.

(*Applause:* JACK *enters with* GOLDIE *and* TICK: *Silence*)

JACK

How come they's no music when I comes in?

CAP'N DAN

How do you do, Mr. Jefferson. As you know, of course,
I am your referee.

JACK

Cap'n Dan, it's a honor.

Ah'm proud to shake the han whut shook
the han of the Prince of Wales.

ROLLER

Don't take that lip from him!

(*General "Ssh"*)

Come on, boog, I'll get it over with right—

(*General hubbub*)

GOLDIE

Colonel—

COX

Quiet down there!

BRADY

Get him on the scale, willya.

JACK (*stepping on*)
Hey, Frank, how you doin?

(BRADY *turns away, muttering*)

Look like Frank bout ta walk de plank!

WEIGHER-IN

One hundred ninety-one.

GOLDIE

Brady?

WEIGHER-IN

Two hundred and four.

TICK

OK, Jack, get down—

JACK

Hey, Frank, you believe that?
This man here saying Ah lighter then you!

BRADY

Yeah, very funny.

CAP'N DAN

Just your statement, please.

JACK

Huh, Oh, sure.
Ah thank Mr. Brady here for bein such a sport,
givin me a shot at the belt today.
They's been plenty a mean talk roun—

(*Jeers*)

COX

Quiet, there—

JACK

But here we is,
an Ah glad it come down to a plain ole scuffle.

(*A few* HANDCLAPS *at the rear of the crowd, which
parts to reveal a* GROUP OF NEGROES *there*)

Mercy me, it's de chillun of Isrel—Hey, there, homefolks!

BRADY

Come on, let's clear out of here—

FRED

Right—

BRADY

Keep rootin, boys—

CROWD

All behind you, Frank—
Kill the coon—
Tear him apart, Frank—
Find that yellow streak—

> (The BAND *strikes up "Hot Time in the Old Town Tonight" as it follows, cheering after* BRADY *and his entourage,* PRESSMEN *and* RANGERS *behind them.* GOLDIE *and* TICK *remain.* JACK *approaches the* GROUP OF NEGROES. *Music and cheering gradually recede)*

JACK

Well, how you all today!

DEACON

Gonna be prayin fo you here, Mr. Jefferson.

JACK

Couldn't get no tickets, huh.

TICK

Bess dey don' go in dere, Jack.

JACK

Yeah, maybe so.

DEACON

That don' matter none. We juss come to pray
you gonna win for us, son.

JACK

Well, if "us" mean any you wid cash ridin on me,
you prayers gonna pay off roun about the fifth.

YOUNG NEGRO

No, Mr. Jefferson. He mean win fo us cullud.

JACK

Oh, that what you prayin!

DEACON

May the good Lawd be guidin your hand for us, son!

ALL NEGROES

Amen, amen.

JACK

An you traipse all this way here to pray it, my, my.

YOUNG NEGRO

What the Revren mean to signify—

JACK

I know what he signify. I big but I ain dumb, hear?

YOUNG NEGRO

What you salty wif me for—

DEACON

We folks just want you to preciate—

JACK (*to* YOUNG NEGRO)

Hey, man. What my winnin gonna do for you!

YOUNG NEGRO

Huh? Oh . . . er . . .

DEACON

Give him self-respeck, that's what!

ALL NEGROES

Amen!

NEGRO 1

Tell it, brother!

YOUNG NEGRO

Yeah—Ah be proud to be a cullud man tomorrow!

NEGROES (*general response*)

Amen, that's it.

JACK
Uh huh.
Well, country boy, if you ain't there already,
all the boxin and nigger-prayin in the world
ain't gonna get you there—

TICK
Jack, let's go—

DEACON
You look cullud, son, but you ain't thinkin cullud.

JACK
Oh, Ah thinkin cullud, cullud and then cullud,
Ah so busy think cullud Ah can't see nothin else some-
    time,
but Ah ain't think cullud-us, like you!
An when you come on wid it, you know what Ah see,
    man?
That ole cullud-us? Juss a basketfulla crabs!
Crabs in a basket—

DEACON
God send you light, son—

GOLDIE
Time to go, Jack—

JACK
Tell me you prayin here! An speck Ah gonna say
Oh, thankya, Revren! You ain't prayin for me!

("*Star Spangled Banner*" in the distance)

It ain't, Lawd, don' let that peck break his nose,
or, Lawd, let him git outa town and not git shot at—
Ah ain nothin in it but a ugly black fiss here!
They don' even push on in to see it workin!

(COLONEL COX reenters)

COX

All set, Jefferson?

JACK (*to the* NEGROES)

Lay your bets, boys, you still got time.

(HE *follows the* COLONEL *out,* GOLDIE *and* TICK *behind him. Lights begin to fade very gradually*)

DEACON

Lawd, when the smoke of the battle clear away here,
may this good strong man be standin up in victry.
May them who keep shovin all us people down
see they can't do it all the time, and take a lesson.
And may us have this livin man today to show us
the sperrit of Joshua. Give this to us, Lawd,
we needs it, and give him light to understand why.

(*The anthem ends and a wolfish cry is heard from the* CROWD *in the stadium*)

NEGRO BOY

Revren—

DEACON

Don' worry, boy. We be all right out here.

(THEY *move back, singing, as the roar increases and the stage darkens*)

NEGROES

(*singing unseen*)
It's so high you can't get over it,
It's so low you can't get under it,
It's so wide you can't get around it,
You must come through by the living gate.

(*The roar reaches a crescendo, suddenly—dies out . . .*

BLACKOUT.

A match lit upstage: CAP'N DAN *in shirt sleeves and braces, lighting a cigar)*

CAP'N DAN *(speaking over his shoulder)*

They better throw away half those pictures they took.
They'll be worse than the fight . . .

(Comes forward)

I really have the feeling
it's the biggest calamity to hit this country
since the San Francisco earthquake—no, I'm serious.
That one at least was only in Frisco.
What kind of calamity? Hard to say it, exactly.
Oh, I don't think all the darkies'll go crazy,
try to take us over, rape and all that.
Be some trouble, yes, but it can be managed—
after all, only one of em's a heavyweight champ . . .
But that's it, I suppose. He is! I hold his hand up,
and suddenly a nigger is Champion of the World!
Now you'll say, Oh, that's only your title in sports—
no, it's more. Admit it. And more than if one got to be
world's best engineer, or smartest politician,
or number one opera singer, or world's biggest genius
at making things from peanuts. No calamity there.
But Heavyweight Champion of the World, well,
it feels like the world's got a shadow across it.
Everything's—no joke intended—kind of darker,
and different, like it's shrinking, it's all
huddled down somehow, and you with it, you want to holler
What's he doin up there,
but you can't because you know . . . that shadow's on you,
and you feel that smile . . .
Well, so what do we do!
Wet our pants, cry in our beer about it?

No, sir, I'll tell you what we do,
we beat those bushes for another White Hope,
and if he's no good we find another White Hope,
we'll find them and we'll boost them up till one stays—
what the hell is this country, Ethiopia?

(BLACKOUT: *music—"Sweet Georgia Brown."* LIGHTS
UP *immediately on—*)

scene four

a street, Chicago.

Dressed-up NEGROES, *more arriving, great animation;
some carry small American flags;* BARKER *among
them with megaphone.* BAND *playing on stage before
an enormous baroque doorway, over which is spelled*
CAFE DE CHAMPION *in lights;* MAN *on ladder installing
the last few bulbs,* ANOTHER *distributing yellow hand-
bills.*

                              BARKER (*through megaphone*)
Every Chicago man, woman, and chile,
you all invited, tan, pink, black, yellow,
and beginner brown, get along down,
let's shake the han of the best in the lan
in his fine new place here, celebrate the openin,
come in you vehicle, come on you foot,
don' bring money, just be here—

(*Auto horns and cheering offstage, then on.* JACK
enters at the wheel of an open white touring-car,
ELLIE *at his side,* TICK *and* GOLDIE *in the rear. A
group of* POLICEMEN *entering with them begins pushing back the* CROWD)

JACK

Hey—hey—they all right, Mistah Offisah,
leave them cullud come on—

(*Cheers as he dismounts and they mill around him,
some with flowers*)

NEGROES

God bless you, Jack—
Ah name mah baby aftuh you—
Member me, Jack?
Ah wish dey wuz ten dozen—
Reach me that han out—

(*The* CLARINETIST *aims an arpeggio at the backs of
the retreating* POLICE: *laughter*)

JACK (*his arms full of flowers*)

Say . . . lookie here, thank you . . . thank you . . . oh
my! . . .
Look like Rest in Peace, don't it!

(*Laughter*)

Well, Ah am all rested up, an like you kin see
Ah bout to make Chicago mah real home sweet home
now—

(*Cheers*)

thass right, permint. Ah don' guess
Ah'll be needin to chase aroun fo work awhile—

(*Laughter*)

an Ah got this joint fix up so's Ah kin visit with mah
frens
an git rich both at once—

(*Laughter, jeers*)

But wait till you see INside—

NEGRO MAN

You ain't stuck Brady's head up on the wall, man, has
you?

(*Hoots, laughter*)

JACK

No, but they's a picture of ole Queen Cleopattera
whut'll make you set straight—

(*Laughter*)

an blue mirrs,
big chambeliers from Germany—well,
Ah ain't gonna spawl it, but say, better tell you,
them jahnt silver pots on the floors, now they artistic,
but they ain't juss for admirin, you know?

(*Laughter. He moves toward the car*)

Tick, you gimme a han with these flowuhs, you too,
Ellie—

(*Silence as she stands to take them, then a spatter of
applause, increasing*)

Yeah, evvybody say hello to mah fiancey, Ellie Bachman!

(*Cheers,* ELLIE *waves, smiling.* TRUMPETER *plays a
bit of* "Here Comes the Bride")

Hole on, don' jump the gun, boy—

(*Laughter*)

An, hey, while you at it,
Gragulate mah manager here, mah fren Goldie—

(*Cheers.* GOLDIE *waves*)

An—

TICK

See? You black, you juss nacheral come in lass—

> (*Laughter.* TICK *springs up, flourishing the gold belt in its plush-lined case*)

Brung this lil doodad, folks, to hang up ovuh de bar!

> (*Whoops, cheers, drum rolls*)

JACK

OK, stash that away now—
What you headin at now
is a special brew a mine in there call Rajah's Peg—
don' ass whut's in it, jes come inside and git it—

> (*Cheers*)

Yeah, open house! Les have some lively times!

> (BAND *strikes up* "Shine." *Cheering continues as* JACK, *cakewalking around the car, ceremoniously collects* ELLIE *and leads her to the doorway, where she formally cuts the ribbon across it; the* NEGROES, *all cakewalking, follow them in, the* BAND *last, continuing to play inside.* GOLDIE *and* TICK *remain*)

TICK

Come on, boss!

GOLDIE

Oh, boy. Oh, boy!
You heard what he said? His fiancée? You heard him?

TICK

Yeah, but dat don' signify nothin—

GOLDIE

Nothin! With bills up in seven states
against any kinda mixed-around marriages!

TICK

Boss, he only juss now say fiancey
so them people don figger she a hooker, thassall—

GOLDIE   **You hear?**

Take a lesson how to be a gentleman!
It's all, he says. Why can't he give them
a chance to boil down, what's he gotta bring her
in the open, for what?

TICK
Juss did it today, boss—

GOLDIE (*gesturing to the car*)
Right down Wabash Avenue—

TICK
                           No law gainst dat yet—

(*Bass drum heard in the distance—continues*)

GOLDIE
What the hell is that?

TICK
I dunno. Muss be some burial society.

(*Enter* SMITTY *and* PRESSMAN 1)

GOLDIE
Go on, take the belt in.

(TICK *goes into the Cafe; cheering, music continuing*)

SMITTY
Lively times, eh, Goldie?

GOLDIE
Yeah. Hiya.

SMITTY

Wouldn't let you in, huh?

GOLDIE

Are you kiddin?

PRESSMAN 1

He came out for some air!

(*They laugh; drum gradually approaching*)

GOLDIE

Look, what's goin on?

SMITTY

They'll be here in a minute, Goldie.

(*Drum very near*)

GOLDIE

They, who's they—?

(*Looks in direction of drumming*)

What the hell is that—?

SMITTY

You know how they are
about places like this. Just their meat, Goldie.

GOLDIE

Oh, Jesus, not here, not down here, I checked it!
Not in this part of town!

SMITTY

Anywhere, Goldie.
It's one big clean-up—

GOLDIE

Oh, boy!

Listen, Smitty, get the cops—

SMITTY

Always cops along, take it easy—

GOLDIE

Smitty—we'll have a riot on our hands here—

SMITTY

Really? I never thought of that.

(*They draw back as a trombone is heard, raggedly joining the drum with "Onward, Christian Soldiers," and the* PARADE *appears, escorted by* POLICEMEN. *The* MARCHERS *carry signs reading:*

CIVIC REFORM NOW
WOMEN'S LEAGUE FOR TEMPERANCE
SEEK YE OUT INIQUITY
AURORA BIBLE COMMITTEE
THOR WITH HIS HAMMER, NORWEGIANS AGAINST SALOONS
HEPWORTH UNION
WE HAVE BEEN TOO PATIENT
CHICAGO JOAN OF ARC CLUBS

A lone NEGRO *among them with a sign:*

NO SPIRITS NO VICE

The music within has stopped. Still playing their anthem, the MARCHERS *range themselves before the doorway. The* NEGROES *within have emerged and stand out before them belligerently.* JACK *comes out as the trombone and drum conclude the anthem*)

MARCHER 1

Woe unto the keepers of the Temples of Baal!
Woe unto the swillers in the sinks of wretchedness!
Woe unto those whose delight is born of evil!

NEGRO 1

Woe whoevuh break up a party on Division Street!

(NEGROES *snarl agreement*)

JACK

Easy now, ace, let the man preach it—

MARCHER 2

We aren't here just to preach, Mr. Jefferson.

WOMAN MARCHER

We tell you to shut this establishment down.

NEGROES

You what?
Who you squeakin at!
Get outa here, fishbait!
Shut me somma this!
Move—

JACK

Easy, easy—now, mistah, lookie here—

NEGROES

Don' argue to em, Jack—
Shoo em off—

WOMAN MARCHER

Shame! Shame, Mr. Jefferson!

MARCHER 1

Instead of offering these people an example—

NEGRO 2 (*squirts a soda
syphon at him*)

Have one on me, chesty!

POLICEMAN 1

Watch it now, you, they got their permit—

JACK

Hey—

NEGRO 2

Don't shove when you talk, man—

MARCHER 1
Drunkenness, disorder, this is what you offer—

NEGRO 3
Do somethin bout it!

MARCHER 1
We shall not allow—

NEGRO WOMAN 1
Stop beatin on de cullud, hear—

POLICEMAN 2
Look—

NEGRO 3
Hands off—

MARCHER 1
We shall not allow fresh corruption to flourish here—

NEGRO 4
I know that mother, I work for him once—

MARCHER 1
We shall not sit by—

NEGRO 3
We ain't gonna let you—

NEGRO WOMAN 1
Stop beatin on de cullud—

NEGRO 2
Show em—

POLICEMAN 3
I warn you—

NEGRO 1
Git de wimmins inside—

MARCHER 1

Sing, friends—

POLICEMAN 1

Keep back—

NEGRO 1

Juss you make one teeny noise—

(ANOTHER NEGRO *breaks through, begins wrestling with the* DRUMMER: *shouting and struggling at the police line*)

JACK

Hey, hey—

MARCHER 1

Hymn number—

NEGRO 2

You ain't hittin no drum here—

WOMAN MARCHER

Help—

(JACK *stops the* POLICE CAPTAIN *from blowing his whistle, then restraining the* NEGRO, *beats the drum with his hand*)

JACK

Order in de court, boys, order in de court!

(*Finally, silence. He picks up the fallen stick and returns it to the* DRUMMER)

Now, you wanta play this ole drum? You play it.

(*To the* MARCHERS)

An you all wanta sing? Then you lean back an sing.

Maybe us kin come in on it, how bout
"Earth Is Not Mah Home, Ah Juss Passin Through"?

(*A few* NEGROES *laugh*)

Thass my favrite.

MARCHER 2
We don't regard this as a frivolous matter, Mr. Jefferson.

JACK
Nossir, me neither! Cause if we kicks off a rumpus
this bran new corruptions a mine here get close up!
Now, I pollgize for any gritty remarks was passed,
an for not bin too symbafetic on you aims—

MARCHER 1
We are going to witness for the Lord—

JACK
OK—

MARCHER 1
On this doorstep as long—

NEGRO 4
Can't sweet-talk em, Jack!

NEGRO WOMAN 1
Always beatin on the cullud!

JACK
Say, is you brains stuck, or what!
These folks been layin down trouble all over,
an here, we's gettin included, ain't we?
Ain't that good enough?
Why, it juss like whut Presden Teddy say,
Square Deal for Evvybody!—come on, les treat em right,
git some chairs out here, they gonna stay, OK,
no use they standin, some old-timie folks
long with em here—

(NEGROES *begin passing chairs out into the street*)]

     Hurry up, they been walkin plenny too,
thass right, Tick, the foldin ones, yeah,
thank you, set em down, couple more, here you go—
if you all want some samwidges or fruit-punch or somethin,
or if, you know, you jus holler out now, OK?
We be right inside—

  (*The intimidated* MARCHERS *have begun moving
 off at the appearance of the chairs, and as the* NE-
 GROES *begin to re-enter the Cafe, two* WHITE MEN *and
 a* WOMAN *enter: They approach* JACK)

      DONNELLY (*the elder of the two*)
Are you Mister Jack Jefferson?

(*All movement ceases*)

      JACK
     Yeah, what about it?

      DONNELLY
My name is Donnelly. I'm an attorney, from Tacoma.
And this is Mrs. Bachman.

(*Pause*)

      JACK
How do you do, ma'am. Would you care to step inside?

      MRS. BACHMAN
No, I would not care to step inside.
Is my daughter in there?

      JACK
     Yes, ma'am. She is.

(DONNELLY *goes in. Silence*)

Ah think she be awful glad to see you, Miz Bachman.

(*Long silence*)

You like to sit down here fo a minute?

(*Long silence*)

Ellie tole me all bout her people back there . . .

(*Silence.* DONNELLY *comes out*)

DONNELLY
She refuses to leave, Mrs. Bachman.

(*Pause*)

MRS. BACHMAN (*crying out*)
Ellie!

(*She crumples, weeping,* DONNELLY *supporting her*)

JACK
She all right, ma'am, she all right, Ah bring her out to
ya—

MRS. BACHMAN (*as* DONNELLY *begins
drawing her away*)
Ellie . . . my baby . . .

GOLDIE
Look, Mister Donnelly, where could I reach you—

DONNELLY
The Majestic—

GOLDIE
OK—

JACK
Ah see she get there—

DONNELLY
You'd better see a little further than that, sir.
I strongly advise you to send that girl home.

(*The beating of the bass drum resumes, as* HE *and the* OTHER MAN, *followed by the* PRESS, *help* MRS. BACHMAN *away; the* MARCHERS *resume their withdrawal, the* NEGROES *returning to the Cafe.* JACK *is last; he turns to* GOLDIE, *now alone on the street*)

GOLDIE
Well ... lively times.

(HE *enters the Cafe as the drumming recedes and the* LIGHTS FADE OUT)

scene five

office of the District Attorney, Chicago.

A meeting in progress. CIVIC LEADERS *facing* CAMERON, *the District Attorney. They include two* WOMEN *and a distinguished-looking* NEGRO. *In the background* SMITTY, *a* DETECTIVE, *and the man with* DONNELLY *in the previous scene:* DIXON.

CAMERON
No, we do not think he's a privileged character!

MAN 1
And still he carries on—

CAMERON

Now wait—

(*Consults papers*)

Since he opened this Cafe, as he calls it,
we have made no fewer than thirteen arrests—

WOMAN 1

He wasn't arrested!

CAMERON

Madam, we have no grounds—

MAN 3

What about that shooting there—

WOMAN 1

You arrested that poor common-law wife of his—

WOMAN 2

He was involved—

CAMERON

Yes, but, madam, SHE shot at HIM!
We can't prosecute him for being a target.

MAN 1

Why isn't action taken about the Bachman girl!

CAMERON

She's over the age of consent, Mr. Hewlett—

MAN 2

This—

(*To the* NEGRO)

Forgive me, Doctor, but I must speak my mind—

This connection between them is an outrage
to every decent Caucasian in America!
Perhaps he thinks his victories entitle him to it,
as part of the spoils—

MAN 1
You know how niggers are—

MAN 2
Mr. Hewlett!

MAN 1 (*to the* NEGRO)
Oh, I'm sorry, sir . . .

NEGRO
We can't pretend that race is not the main issue here.
And, as you imply, sir, the deportment of this man
does harm to his race. It confirms certain views of it
you may already hold: that does us harm.
But it also confirms in many Negroes the belief
that his life is the desirable life, and that
does us even greater harm. **For a Negro today,
the opportunity to earn a dollar in a factory
should appear to be worth infinitely more
than the opportunity of spending that dollar
in emulation of Mr. Jack Jefferson.**
But this I assert: the majority of Negroes
do not approve of this man or of his doings.
He personifies all that should be suppressed by law,
and I trust that such suppression is forthcoming.

(*General agreement*)

MAN 2
Everyone in favor say aye—

ALL
Aye!

(THEY *rise,* CAMERON *with them*)

CAMERON

Well, I appreciate your coming here to discuss this—

MAN 2

It will not be to your benefit to let it rest here.

CAMERON

I don't intend to, sir.

(*Sees* THEM *out*)

Good night, good night.

(HE *shuts the door.* SMITTY, DIXON, *and* DETECTIVE *come forward*)

DETECTIVE

Like a drink?

CAMERON

Sure could use one.

(*Bottle is produced,* DIXON *abstains*)

Smitty?

SMITTY

I'm in training.

CAMERON

You know . . . if a good White Hope showed up and beat him
it would take the edge off this.

SMITTY

Forget it, Al.
The best we got around now is Fireman Riley.

CAMERON

All right, let's go to work. Bring the girl in.

(DETECTIVE *leaves*)

You want to question her, Dixon? It was your idea.

DIXON

No, you go ahead, Al. See what you can come up with.

SMITTTY

Why don't you revoke the license on his place,
that's easy enough.

CAMERON
Sure it's easy!
We could close him, we could rap him on disorderly
     conduct,
we could make a dozen misdemeanors stick,
but it's all minor stuff. And you heard them.
They want his head on a plate.

(DETECTIVE *enters with* ELLIE)

Good evening, Miss Bachman. Take a seat, please.

ELLIE

Thank you.

(DIXON, SMITTY, *and* DETECTIVE *withdraw into the
background*)

CAMERON

You understand, this is an informal inquiry,
you've come at our request, but of your own free will?

ELLIE

Yes, I understand.

CAMERON

Good. Now, Miss Bachman—

(*Consulting papers*)

Yes, I see.
You resumed your maiden name after your divorce.

ELLIE

That's right.

CAMERON

And you obtained your divorce from Mr. Martin in
Australia.

ELLIE

Yes.

CAMERON

An odd place to go for a divorce.

ELLIE

I have an aunt there. I wanted to get away.

CAMERON

You hadn't met Mr. Jefferson before your trip.

ELLIE

No, I had not.

CAMERON

You did not travel there to be with Mr. Jefferson.

ELLIE

No, I did not. I met him on the boat.

CAMERON

How did he approach you?

ELLIE

He didn't. I asked the captain to introduce us.

CAMERON

May I ask why.

ELLIE

Yes. I wanted to make his acquaintance.

CAMERON

And once you had, Miss Bachman, what did he propose to you?

ELLIE

That I have dinner at his table.

CAMERON

Which you did for several evenings—

ELLIE

Yes—

CAMERON

Until you began taking your meals in his stateroom.

ELLIE

That is correct.

CAMERON (*consulting papers*)

Where a great deal of wine and champagne was consumed.

ELLIE

You might say that.

CAMERON

Presumably he would keep filling your glass . . . ?

ELLIE

When it was empty, yes.

CAMERON

Ten times per evening? Six?

ELLIE

No, I drank very little—

CAMERON
And how often did he give you
medicine or pills—

ELLIE
Never, I wasn't ill—

CAMERON
But the steward reports that you hardly left the stateroom,
and that disembarking you appeared quite—

ELLIE
Well, the last day at sea we had—

CAMERON
Weren't you ill in some way?
Did you feel strange, or sleepy—

ELLIE
I felt uncomfortable at how people looked at me.
I wasn't used to it.

CAMERON
He took you from the boat to the hotel.

ELLIE
Yes.

CAMERON
Did you ask to be taken there?

ELLIE
No, I just went with him.

CAMERON
And what had he promised you?

ELLIE
To spend some of his time with me.

CAMERON

Nothing else?

ELLIE

Nothing that could interest you.

CAMERON

But naturally, since you were staying there with him, he provided you with money.

ELLIE

I have Mr. Martin's settlement and means of my own. He's given me presents, yes—

DIXON

Miss Bachman,
Your railway ticket to Chicago,
did you buy it yourself? Or was it a sort of present.

ELLIE

I honestly don't remember. Yes, I believe I bought it.

DIXON

Thank you.

CAMERON

You're parrying these questions very well!

ELLIE

I didn't come here to tell lies, Mr. Cameron.
I agreed to come, though Jack was against it,
because I wanted to head off any notions you have
of getting at him through me. I hope I've done that.

CAMERON (*putting away papers*)

Well . . . it seems you have. And frankly I admire you for it.
Not many women . . . yes, one has to.

(*Sits on desk*)

You're quite devoted to him, aren't you?

ELLIE
I love him, Mr. Cameron.

CAMERON
                    He's a splendid man
in many ways, really. No one doubts that, you know.

ELLIE
I've never doubted it.

CAMERON
A magnificent fighter. I saw him when he—

ELLIE
That's not all he is. He's generous, he's kind,
he's sensitive—why are you smiling?

CAMERON
I'm sorry. It's how you shy away from mentioning
the physical attraction. I've embarrassed you, forgive
    me—

ELLIE
I'm not ashamed of wanting Jack for a lover.
I wanted him that way.

CAMERON
                    Of course you did,
and of course he'd want you!

ELLIE
                    Why, because I'm—

CAMERON
Oh no, I'm not implying—

ELLIE

He could have nearly any girl he wanted, black or—

CAMERON

Yes, I only meant that any man would be proud—

ELLIE

I'm proud that he wanted me! Is that clear?

CAMERON

Certainly—please don't be distressed, we needn't—

ELLIE

Who am I, anyway! I'm no beauty or anything or—

CAMERON

Now, now, you're being unfair to yourself—

ELLIE

Why can't they leave us alone, what's the difference—

(SHE *weeps*)

CAMERON

Oh, there shouldn't be one, ideally . . . and besides,
people are so blind about that physical side—
a young woman, divorced, disappointed—

ELLIE

Please. If you've finished—

CAMERON

Here, here, now, you mustn't cry, Miss Bachman,
it hasn't turned out all that badly, has it?
You have this wonderful man now to love you—
why should you cry—

ELLIE

I'll never give him up, I can't—

CAMERON

Of course not, but why be ashamed of it—

ELLIE

I'm not, I swear I'm not—

CAMERON

You seem to be, you know—

ELLIE

I'm not—

CAMERON

Well, if you say so—

ELLIE

I'm crazy for him, yes! I don't care! It's the truth!
I didn't know what it was till I slept with him!
I'll say it to anyone, I don't care how it sounds—

CAMERON

That he makes you happy that way—

ELLIE

Yes—

CAMERON

And you love him, you'd do anything for him—?

ELLIE

Yes—

CAMERON

And not be ashamed—?

ELLIE

No, never—

CAMERON

Even if it—

ELLIE

Yes—

CAMERON

Seemed unnatural or—

ELLIE

Yes—

CAMERON

And when you have, you only—

ELLIE

What—?

CAMERON

Tried to make him happy too, am I right?

(SHE *freezes. Pause*)

Now, Miss Bachman—

ELLIE *(with Negro inflection)*

You slimy two-bit no-dick mothergrabber.

(*Pause.* SHE *rises*)

If that's all.

CAMERON

Yes, I believe so—

ELLIE

Good night, then.

CAMERON

Yes. Thank you for coming in.

(*Sees her out, shuts the door*)

SMITTY

That's that.

CAMERON

Nothing!
Seduction, enticement, coercion, abduction,
not one good berry on the bush!

DETECTIVE

Too bad, Al.
Nearly did get him on five seventy-one, though.

CAMERON

Rah!

SMITTY

Makes your hair stand up, don't it?

DETECTIVE

Sure does.
She's like a kid with a piece of chocolate cake.

CAMERON

All right! It's a rotten job . . . !

(*To* DIXON)

So, what do you think?
Any hope of a Federal slap here?

DIXON

I'm not sure yet, Al.
I'll need to have a word with the fine-print boys.
And I'd like to speak to Donnelly—OK?

(DETECTIVE *leaves*)

CAMERON

But what's there to move on? The railway ticket?

DIXON

Well, maybe not that, exactly.
I doubt if we could prove he actually bought it—

CAMERON

And say you could—so?

DIXON

            It's occurred to me, Al—
seeing how we've just drawn a blank everywhere else—
that we might just nail him with the Mann Act.

CAMERON

                                                What?
But that's for commercial ass, not this. She's not a pro!

DIXON

Yes, I know that, Al. But here is a law against
"transporting a person across a state line
for immoral purposes."

CAMERON

                No riders, nothing
about "intent to gain" or "against volition"?

DIXON

I don't believe so.

    (DONNELLY *enters with* DETECTIVE)

            Oh, good evening, Mr. Donnelly.
We've spoken to your young lady—

DONNELLY

                        Yes? And—?

DIXON

You'll remember that our office agreed, at the outset,
not to involve her in any proceedings
unless it was absolutely necessary.

Unfortunately, now, Mr. Donnelly, it may be,
and we shall probably require certain evidence.
We thought you should know this beforehand, so that
   you
may return to Tacoma and prepare your principal.

                    DONNELLY
I understand, sir.

                    DIXON
           Good. Thank you.

                    CAMERON
I'll have that bastard watched day and night!

                    DIXON
Don't bother, Al. We've done it right along.

   (BLACKOUT. *Sound of crickets chirping.* LIGHTS UP
   on—)

scene six

a cabin, Beau Rivage, Wisconsin.

ELLIE *sitting up in bed, a sheet around her.* JACK,
wrapped in a towel, beside her. Kerosene lamp.

                    JACK
Shucks, honey, it ain't cold, this the finest time for
   swimmin—

                    ELLIE
We have come to a parting of the ways.

JACK

Aw ... big silvery moon, pine trees—

ELLIE

Snapping turtles, moccasins—

JACK

Lawd, whut to do when romance done gone!

ELLIE

Oh, Jack, I couldn't make it to the door.

JACK

That right? Sposin Ah carry you down there then
an sorta—

ELLIE

No—

JACK

Ease you in—

ELLIE

No! No fair—Jack!—don't tickle me—

JACK

Mmm, she a reglah—

ELLIE

Please—no!—Ow!—Jack, that hurts—

JACK

Hey, baby, Ah didn—

ELLIE

I know, this damn sunburn.

JACK

Aw, Ah'm sorry—here, lemme pat somethin on it—

(*Takes up a champagne bottle, applies some to her back*)

Yeah ...

ELLIE

Oh, thanks ... ooh ... oh, yes, it's—Jack?

JACK

Don' that feel good now?

ELLIE

What are—?

JACK

Cool—?

ELLIE

Not champagne, Jack!

JACK

Well, thass alright, baby, you worth the bess.

ELLIE

All over me ...

JACK

Get some lake on you, huh?

ELLIE

No, I—

(*Peering at him*)

Jack, turn around a little ...
more, this way ... Are you feeling all right?

JACK

Ah ain't feelin no diffrunt.

ELLIE

Are you sure?

JACK

Yeah!

ELLIE

You ate all those clams, maybe you—

(*Feels his head*)

JACK

Whut you doin that for, ain't got no fever—

ELLIE

Well, you look—a little peculiar, Jack.

JACK

Oh . . . ? Kinda ashy, you mean?

ELLIE

Yes, a sort of funny—

JACK

Honey, that ain't sick, that how Ah gets a sunburn.

(ELLIE *tries not to laugh*)

Now what you laughin at—

ELLIE

I thought—I mean—oh!—oh, Jack—

JACK

Huh?

ELLIE

I can't help it, I'm sorry—how you—oh—

JACK

Yeah—come on, that ain't nice—

(HE *starts to laugh*)

You thought what, honey?

ELLIE

I—I thought it just—bounces off, that's all—

(BOTH *laugh uproariously*)

JACK

Bounces off—

ELLIE

Yes—

JACK

Well, Miss Medium Rare, meet Mr. Well Done!

(*Gales of laughter*)

Yeah . . . lotta folks better off in de shade.

ELLIE

Oh . . . do we have to leave tomorrow?

JACK

Shouldn't leave the place alone too long, honey.

ELLIE

I know. All right.

JACK

Case there's any fussin or—

ELLIE

Ssh, I know.

JACK

My, you do smell good though.

ELLIE

Yes?

JACK

Mm-hmm.

ELLIE

You're not tired of being alone with me, are you?

JACK

Hey. You kiddin?

ELLIE

Or tired of me asking questions like that?

JACK

Oh . . . Ah'm gettin tired of plenny . . . but, no, you ain't in there at' all.

ELLIE

It's lovely to hear you say that . . .

JACK

Yeah? . . . Well, OK then . . .

(*Props himself up*)

How you doin for pillers?

ELLIE

Fine, darling . . .

(JACK *hums a little*)

Have a swim if you want to.

JACK

No, Ah'm cozy here . . . I cozy, an you rosy . . .

> (ELLIE *chuckles.* JACK *turns the lamp down very low,
> kisses her, draws away. Sings softly*)

> Good morning, blues
> Blues, how do you do,
> Blues say, Ah all right,
> Brother, how are you.
> Woke up dis mornin,
> Blues all round mah head,
> Look down to mah breakfas,
> Blues all in mah bread . . .
> For how long, how long,
> Ah sayin, how long . . .

ELLIE

Lying in the sun I was, you know, daydreaming . . .
how maybe I'd stay there . . . and it would keep on
  burning me . . .
day after day . . . oh, right through September . . .
And I'd get darker and darker . . . I really get dark, you
  know . . .
and then I'd dye my hair . . . and I'd change my name . . .
and I'd come to you in Chicago . . . like somebody
  new . . .
a colored woman, or a Creole maybe . . .
and nobody but you would ever guess . . .

JACK

Won't work, honey.

ELLIE

Hm?

JACK

Evvybody know Ah gone off cullud women.

ELLIE

Oh, Jack, don't tease . . .

JACK

Ah has, too, 'cep for mah momma.

ELLIE

Maybe if I . . .

JACK

Ssh.

ELLIE

What will we do . . .

JACK

Ssh . . . try an sleep, honey . . .

(*Turns the lamp down a little further*)

Creepin up on me a little too—

(*Darkness. Sings*)

For how long, how long, Ah sayin . . .
Always callin you honey, ain't Ah.

ELLIE

Mm.

JACK

Don' remember Ah call no woman by that.
Call em by their name . . . or juss "baby," you know . . .
Don' ever call you by you name, Ah guess . . .

ELLIE

Hardly ever . . .

JACK

Muss be some kinda ju-ju Ah fraid of in it . . .
like if Ah says it you maybe disappear on me . . .

ELLIE

Oh . . . I don't care about my name . . .

JACK

Honey . . . hit just right . . .

ELLIE

Yes . . .

JACK

Honey fum the bees . . .

(SHE *sighs*)

Ever look at it real, real good a while . . . ?

ELLIE

Can't remember . . .

JACK
               Nothin like that stuff . . .
Used to sit . . . Oh, long time ago, it Texas . . .
we-all ud have a lil honey-treat sometime . . .
whole yellah mugful . . . used to set there with it
till evvybody come in . . . foolin with it, you know . . .
liff up a spoonful . . . tip it a lil bit . . .
watch it start to curve up . . . start in
to sli-i-i-de ovuh . . . oh, takin its time . . . slow . . .
   slow . . .
honey underneath waitin . . . honey hanging ovuh it . . .
hundred years up there . . . then down . . . stringing
   down . . . down . . .
tiny lil dent where it touch . . . an then . . .

   (*Suddenly embracing her*)

Oh, mah sweet, sweet baby, Ah want to have it all—

ELLIE

Yes—

(*Sound of a door splintered open.* SIX MEN—*two with lanterns—burst in. Confusion of light and bodies*)

MAN 1

On your feet, Jefferson—

ELLIE

Jack—

MAN 2

Get the window, Charlie—

MAN 3

Hey—

MAN 1

Look out—

MAN 4

Oh!

MAN 5

Grab him—

MAN 4

He's—chokin me—

MAN 1

Here, you—

(*Thud.* ELLIE *screams*)

MAN 1

Let go or I'll put a hole in you—

MAN 2

Where is he—

MAN 1

I said—

(*Thud*)

ELLIE

Stop it—

MAN 4

Jesus—

MAN 6

Light that goddamn lamp—

ELLIE

Please—

MAN 5

Sit there, lady—

MAN 1

We're the law.

(*Kerosene lamp on.* ELLIE *huddled at the head of the bed,* JACK *crouching in a corner, grasping a chunk of firewood, the injured* MAN *nursing his neck, the* OTHERS *facing* JACK, *immobile—*DIXON *is among them,* ALL *breathing heavily.* DIXON *moves forward*)

DIXON

I'm a federal marshal, Jefferson.

(*Shows his badge*)

　　　　　　　　　　　Put that down, please.

(*Pause*)

Come on. We don't want to make this any worse.

(*Pause.* JACK *drops wood*)

At ten A.M. this morning you drove Miss Eleanor Bach-
　　man
across the Illinois-Wisconsin state line.

Having done so, you proceeded to have relations with
    her.
Under the Mann Act this makes you liable
and I'm therefore placing you under arrest.

ELLIE

No . . . no . . .

DIXON

Get dressed, please, Miss Bachman. We'll take you into
    town.

ELLIE

Jack—

JACK

Don't worry—get dress—

    (*Handing her her clothes*)

MAN 2

Here.

DIXON

Hold a blanket up or something.

ELLIE

Jack . . .

JACK

Don't you fret now . . .

    (MAN 2 *and* MAN 3 *screen her with a blanket. To*
    DIXON)

Thanks, mistah.

DIXON

Sure.

JACK (*pulling on a sweater*)

How much this carry?

DIXON

One to three.

JACK

She clear?

DIXON

Just you.

JACK

Yeah. Thanks.

MAN 1 (*showing handcuffs*)

We need these, Jim?

DIXON

No. Find him his pants and let's get out of here.

(BLACKOUT.
*Soft, woeful singing in the darkness, which contin-
ues through the following. A bizarre-looking colored
man comes forward:* SCIPIO. HE *wears a shabby purple
cloak fastened with a gold clasp over a shabby dark
suit, a bowler hat with a long plume hanging from
it, fawn shoes, and several large totemic-looking
rings. His manner is feverish*)

SCIPIO (*speaking over his
shoulder into the
darkness*)

Start it up, thassit, brothers, singing and moanin!
White man juss drag him another away here
so all you black flies, you light down together
an hum pretty please to white man's Jesus—
Yes, Lawd!

(*Spits*)

Waste a mah times . . .
An Ah don' care to talk to you neither!
But Ah sees two-three out there de same blood is me,
so Ah says good-evenin to em, then Ah askin em this:
How much white you up to? How much you done took
    on?
How much white you pinin for? How white you wanna
    be?
Oh, mebbe you done school youself away fum White
    Jesus—
but how long you evah turn you heart away frum
    WHITE!
How you lookin, how you movin, how you wishin an
    figgering—
how white you wanna be, that whut Ah askin!
How white you gaunta get—you tell me!
You watchin that boy? Nothin white-y bout him, huh?
But whut he hustle after? White man's sportin prize!
Whut he gotta itch for? White man's poontang!
Whut his rich livin like? White man's nigger!
Thinks he walkin and talkin like a natchul man,
don' know how he's swimmin half-drownded in the
    whitewash,
like they is, like you is, nevah done diffrunt,
gulpin it in evvy day, pickled in it, right at home dere—
tell me that ain't how we living!
Tell me how it better you chokin on dat whitewash
than wearin a iron colluh roun you neck!
Oh, yeah, you sayin, but whut kin we do,
Whut kin us or dat boy or dem gospellers do,
we passin our days in de white man's world—well,
make you own, brothers!
Don' try an join em an don' try an beat em,
leave em all at once, all together,
pack up!
Colleck you wages, grab whutevah here gonna come in
    handy
an sluff off de ress! Time to get it goin!
Time again to make us

a big new wise proud dark man's world
again! Ah says again! Ah tellin what we had once!
Nevah mine that singing—learn, brothers, learn!
Ee-gyp!! Tambuctoo!! Ethiopya!!
Red'n goldin cities older den Jeruslem,
temples an prayin to sperrits whut stick wid us,
black men carvin ivory, workin up laws,
chartin em maps for de moon an de sun,
refine' cultured cullud people hansome as statues dere
when Europe an all was juss woods fulla hairy canni-
    bals—
dat laughin don' harm us none!
Five hundrid million of us not all together,
not matchin up to em, dat what harmin us!
Dream bout it, brothers—
Five hundrid million on dey own part of de earth,
am not a one dere evah askin another,
How much white you up to,
how white you wanna be . . .

(*Glaring,* HE *makes his exit as* LIGHTS COME UP *on—*)

scene seven

Mrs. Jefferson's house, Chicago.

Surrounding MRS. JEFFERSON *in her armchair are the*
PASTOR *and seven or eight* BROTHERS *and* SISTERS,
who continue singing softly, as the PASTOR *speaks.*
At one side is CLARA, *now dressed rather plainly.*
MRS. JEFFERSON *wears a nightdress, with a shawl over*
her shoulders and another covering her legs.

PASTOR

Lawd, we prayin longside this sick unhappy mother here,
she lookin to You, Lawd, she know her boy been sinful,
an she sorry about that, but she do love him, Lawd,
you give him another chance she nevah ask you for anythin!
She living by You Book all her days, Lawd, you seen it!
We prayin you touch them judges' eyes with mercy.
Let em chastise him today, Lawd,
let em fine him so steep he leff withouta dime,
let em scare him so hard he nevah forgit it,
but, Lawd, don' let em lock this woman's boy away.

(*End singing*)

BROTHERS

Amen.

MRS. JEFFERSON

An if they does, Oh please, Lawd, let it juss be fo a little.

BROTHERS

Amen.

PASTOR

We callin with you, sister.

MRS. JEFFERSON

Ah thank ya, Pastor.
Wish Ah could offuh ya some lil hospitality
but honess—

PASTOR

Don' fret now, sister.

MRS. JEFFERSON

Ah mean, Ah kin hardly—

> SISTER 1
> Nevah you mine, Tiny.

> CLARA

Ah'll put on a potta fresh cawfee—

(Starts to go)

> MRS. JEFFERSON

See if Tick or somebody comin down the street firss.

(CLARA goes to the window)

> SISTER 2

Early yet, sister.

> CLARA

Juss a buncha fellers there gawnta play baseball.

> MRS. JEFFERSON *(sighs)*

Awright, Clara. Thankya.

> PASTOR *(as CLARA goes to
> kitchen)*

Got a guardjin angel with that gal in you house.

> BROTHER 1

Who deserve one better!

(BROTHERS approve)

> MRS. JEFFERSON

Should've brung word by this. Caint've took this long.

> PASTOR

We in de Lawd's hans, sister.

> BROTHERS
> Amen.

SISTER 1
You sit easy . . .

MRS. JEFFERSON
Fum when he was chile Ah knowed this day comin.
Looka that, Momma, why cain't Ah, Momma,
lemme lone, Momma. Nevah stop. Fidgety feet
an, oh, them great big eyes, roamin an reachin, all ovuh.
Tried to learn him like you gotta learn a cullud boy,
Dass'nt, dass'nt, dass'nt, that ain't for you!
Roll right off him. Tried to learn it to him meaner—
Mo chile you got, the meaner you go to
if you lovin you chile. That plain cullud sense.
Hit him with my han, he say, So what.
Hit him with my shoe, he look up an smile.
Took a razor-strop to him, that make him squint
but then he do a funny dance an ask me fo a nickel.
Ah prayed to de Lawd put mo strenf in my arm,
the worse Ah was whippin the bigger he growed,
leven years old an still woulden hear nothin.
Hit him with a stick till Ah coulden hit no mo,
he pull it away fum me, an bust it in two,
an then he run off—

PASTOR
Sister—

MRS. JEFFERSON
Lawd fogive me treatin him so mean!
Lawd fogive me not beatin on him young enough
or hurtin him bad enough to learn him after,
cause Ah seen this day comin—

(*Knock downstairs*)

SISTER 1
Ah let em in, Tiny.

(*Goes*)

PASTOR

We hopin with you, sister. Hole onter my han now.

MRS. JEFFERSON

No, thass awright.

SISTER 1 (*offstage*)

But you all muss ain't got de right house—

RUDY (*offstage*)

Two thirty-one?

TEAMMATE (*offstage*)

Miz Jeffson's house, ain't it?

SISTER 1 (*closer*)

Yeah, but—hang on, whole lotta you cain't fit here—

RUDY

OK, set on de stairway, de ress of you—

(SISTER 1 *backs into the room, followed by three large* YOUNG NEGROES *wearing blue satin jackets and matching baseball caps.* THEY *carry valises from which bats and other gear protrude. Their leader, and the largest,* RUDY, *takes off his cap and the* OTHERS *follow suit.* CLARA *re-enters from the kitchen*)

Aftuhnoon, evvybody.

MRS. JEFFERSON

You all comin fum de courthouse?

RUDY

No ma'am. Us juss get a message—uh—
askin we pay a call here. We de Blue Jays.

MRS. JEFFERSON

You de which?

RUDY

De-troit Blue Jays. You know, de cullud baseball club?
Pulvrise de Afro Giants here Sadday?

BROTHER 2

Oh, yeah, my nephew tend dat game.

RUDY

My name Rudy Sims, ma'am.

MRS. JEFFERSON

Pleased to meet you, Mistah Sims—

CLARA

Who say you sposeta call in here?

RUDY

Well, we sorta frens with Jack—

CLARA

This here no celebratin party, you know!

MRS. JEFFERSON

Hush, Clara, if they frens with Jack—

CLARA

Why somebody sen us a baseball team here!

RUDY

Mebbe we bess wait outside in de hall, ma'am—

MRS. JEFFERSON

Nothin of the kine! Clara—

CLARA

Ah ain't never seed Jack wid no baseball frens!

(TICK *enters*)

RUDY

Well, Ah nevuh seed him wid you, so we even.

TICK

Don' let her rile you, Rudy. Thanks for comin.

RUDY

Any time, man.

TICK

Got here fass as I could, Miz Jeffson.

MRS. JEFFERSON

Well. You here ... Come on.

TICK

It ain't good, Miz Jeffson.

SISTER 1

Lawd have mercy.

MRS. JEFFERSON

Come on. Finish up.

TICK

Twenty-thousand-dollar fine and three years in Joliet.

SISTER 2

Jesus above.

BROTHER 1

Three years.

CLARA

Why cain't all dem Jew lawyers do nothin! Why cain't—

TICK

Dey got a week ta try appealin on it—

BROTHER 1

Three years.

MRS. JEFFERSON

Ah die they lock him up!

SISTER 2

Don' take on, sister—

PASTOR

Bring me them smellin salts—

SISTER 1

Tiny—

MRS. JEFFERSON

No, Ah don' want nothin—

TICK

He do have de week out on bail, Miz Jeffson—
dey set it kina heavy but we figgered dey might,
an we gonna make it.

MRS. JEFFERSON

A week. Drive him crazy!

TICK

Well, we gotta try an see it don't.

CLARA

That snaky lil wax-face bitch! Where she at now!
Where she bloodsuckin now! Oh, Ah'll smoke her out,
an, man—

PASTOR

Sister—

CLARA

What Ah gonna do
be worth a hunnerd three yearses!

MRS. JEFFERSON

Ain't her fault, Clara.

CLARA

She knowd this end-up comin,

ain a deaf dumb bline pinhead living din know it,
but, Oh, daddy, she joyin hersel so,
it so good when it goin! Leave it alone?
Oh, but, daddy, Ah loves you!

MRS. JEFFERSON

Could be she do love him, Clara.

CLARA
                    She WHAT!

MRS. JEFFERSON

He brung her down once. She din seem too bad.

TICK

Nice an quiet too.

CLARA
                Ah ain't talkin to you!
Could be she love him! Why she scat off
wid her man in trouble, why she—

PASTOR

Bess unwine dat serpint from you heart, sister—

CLARA

Love him, my black ass!

PASTOR
                Sister!

MRS. JEFFERSON (*as* CLARA *returns
                    to kitchen*)

Poor gal been frettin so—

(JACK *and* GOLDIE *enter*)

PASTOR

Praise de Lawd an welcome.

JACK

Pastor . . . evvybody . . . good boy, Rudy.

RUDY

Ready fo ya, Jack.

JACK

Fine, no rush . . . hiya, Momma Tiny.

MRS. JEFFERSON

They din hurt you, Jack? You git nuff to eat?

JACK

Sure, Momma.

GOLDIE

I should feel as good as he does.

JACK

Whut about you, Momma?

MRS. JEFFERSON

Oh . . .

JACK

Still kina poorly?

MRS. JEFFERSON

It drain me out some, Ah guess.

JACK

Oh, Momma.

BROTHER 2

Hard luck, Jack.

MRS. JEFFERSON

We been prayin an prayin here, son.

JACK

Well . . . de Lawd hear anyone he gonna hear you.

MRS. JEFFERSON

Look like he ain't this time—
but He gonna put me on my feet, Ah kin feel it!
An Ah gonna help Him, gonna ress up an eat good,
an Ah comin down there soon, Jack—

JACK

       Momma—

MRS. JEFFERSON

Often as they 'low ya to, you wait an see,
bring a big ole picnic basket on my arm—

JACK

       No, Momma, listen—

CLARA (*flinging herself
    upon him*)

Oh, baby, baby, Ah cain't let em clap you in there—

JACK

What she doin here!

GOLDIE

That's all we need.

JACK

Git offa me, you! Momma, whut de hell—

MRS. JEFFERSON

Clara come roun when she hear Ah was ailin—

CLARA

Ah been doin fo you momma, Jack—

MRS. JEFFERSON

She tryna menn her ways—

> TICK (*stealing a look
> out of window*)
> Jack.

(JACK *looks at him.* HE *nods. Pause*)

> JACK (*to* CLARA)
Ah count ten fo you to beat it. One—

> CLARA

No!

> MRS. JEFFERSON

She been my helpmeet, Jack!

> JACK

Sister fine ya a housekeeper!

> CLARA

Ah keepin house, baby!

> JACK

Ah up to five, girl—

> TICK (*tense. At the window*)
> Let her be for now, Jack.

She in here she cain't spoil it,
screamin in the street or somethin.

> GOLDIE (*mopping his face*)
> That's all we need.

> RUDY

Soun like sense, Jack.

> MRS. JEFFERSON

Spoil what? Mistah, what these boys up to?

> BROTHER 1

Yeah, what goin on here?

CLARA (*to* TICK *at window*)
Whuffo you playin peekaboo wid dat dere automo-bile?

(HE *shoos her away*)

PASTOR (*to* JACK)
You ain't about to make things worse, son, are you?

MRS. JEFFERSON
Jack—

JACK
Awright. I gotta truss all you folks now—

PASTOR
Son, however rough it 'pears today—

TICK
Oughta stan by the winder now, Jack. They lookin.

MRS. JEFFERSON
Who? Who lookin?

JACK
'Tectives in that car, Momma.

MRS. JEFFERSON
Jack—

JACK
Momma, listen—

MRS. JEFFERSON
What they waitin out there for, Mistah Goldie?

GOLDIE
Well, even though Jack is out on bond, you see—

JACK
They worried Ah gonna try an jump mah bail, Momma.

GOLDIE
They're worried. I'm in hock up to here with this.

MRS. JEFFERSON
Jack . . . you juss got let out.

JACK
Bess time, Momma. They don' know Ah's ready.

MRS. JEFFERSON
They follerin you, but!

JACK
Thinks they is.

MRS. JEFFERSON
Jack, what if they catches you—

JACK
Won't never get near me! Now, firss thing what Ah do
is take my coat off—

(*Does so, revealing a raspberry-colored shirt*)

then I stan here sorta talkin—
"Why heaven sake, no foolin!"—now let em see mah
face—

(*Looks out*)

"Oh, my, it look like rain . . ."—an Ah knows they seen
my shirt—
Mm-mm! Don't you wish you had one!
Well, Ah goes on talkin, right? Now over there is Rudy—

(RUDY *looks at his watch*)

Uh-oh, he checkin his turnip again!
They hasta hop on the train soon, you know,
Blue Jays playin Montreal nex, ain't you, Rude,
gainst de Canada Blacks?

RUDY
Thass right, Jack.

JACK
Less go, fellah—

(RUDY *starts peeling off jacket and jersey*)

He look mighty fine, ole Rude here, don' he!
Not pretty is me, but he near is big
an just a half shade blacker an—
Oh, mercy, he got dat shirt on too!

(RUDY *does*)

SISTER 1
Lawd proteck us!

JACK (*looks out*)
"Yeah, it clearin up now—"

GOLDIE
Jack, listen, we should maybe talk it over more—

MRS. JEFFERSON (*to* GOLDIE)
What you trick him inter!

GOLDIE
It's his idea, believe me—

JACK
It be awright, Momma!
Rudy spen de aftuhnoon by the winder
an Ah go rollin cross de border with de Jays!

BROTHER 2
They fine you out, Jack—

JACK
Naw! I put on Rudy's cap an his jacket?
Stick in the middle of his boys?

Who all fine me! An who lookin?
You hear that sayin how all niggers look alike!
Ain't that so, team?

PASTOR

But, son, you fogittin we frens with that Canada!
I mean, we's hardly a diffrunt place—

TICK

Fore they cotton to it, man,
We on dat ole boat fo Englin. Right?

GOLDIE

Right, right.

JACK

It all fixed, Momma!

MRS. JEFFERSON

All what fixed ain't gotta juss happen—

PASTOR

Serious offense to go floutin de law, Jack!
I know they done you real hard but, son,
it gonna hang ovuh you long as—

JACK
                Look!
What hang gonna hang but Ah ain't hangin with it!
Ah done my kickin roun this country,
Ah serve my one nights and my thirty days too once,
an Ah ain't gonna rot like no log no three years!
Or be comin out broke as Ah is now either!
Ah in the prime of mah life! Ah wanna live like Ah
    got to,
wanna make me some money again, wanna fight!
Ah got my turn to be Champeen of the World
an Ah takin my turn! Ah stayin whut Ah am,
wherever Ah has to do it!
The world ain't curled up into no forty-eight states here!

MRS. JEFFERSON

Praise de Lawd for lightin a way fo my boy!
Fogive me Ah say Ah didden love you, Jesus!

JACK (*moving to her*)

Thassit, Momma—

MRS. JEFFERSON (*to* BROTHERS
and PASTOR)
Well?

BROTHERS & PASTOR (*worried*)
Amen . . .

GOLDIE

She could put in a word for me too, here.

RUDY (*taking his place at
the window*)
Better move it, man.

JACK
Right.

(*Pulls on* RUDY'S *jersey*)

GOLDIE
Oh, boy.

JACK

You folks stay here till we gone, OK?
Then start runnin in an out like, keep em busy watchin—

CLARA

Oh, take me with you, honey—

JACK (*pulls on a jacket*)
Don't you cross me now—

CLARA

Ah go meet you, baby! Any place!

JACK

You know the score, girl.

CLARA

Please!

JACK (*buttoning up*)

Fit awright?

GOLDIE

Yeah, beautiful.

CLARA

She comin to ya, ain't she! That where she at!

JACK

Hope you gettin to that game on time, Rudy—

CLARA

You ain't meetin that bitch! I turn you in firss—

(*Runs at the door*)

TICK

Hole her—

CLARA (*shaking loose from him*)

JACK GONNA—

(*Struggles with* SISTERS *at the door*)

SISTER 1

Stop her mouf up—

CLARA

HE RUNNIN FFFF—

(*Stopping her mouth,* THEY *drag her from the door, kicking*)

GOLDIE

Oh, boy—

BROTHER 1

Make some noise!

SISTER 2

Sit on her—

PASTOR

"Look ovuh, Beulah—"

BROTHER 2

Which—?

PASTOR

Ready—

MRS. JEFFERSON

No "Beulah" now, sen up a glad one—

SISTER 1

Quick, she bitin me—

MRS. JEFFERSON

Sing, chillun—

ALL (*but* CLARA, *on whom the three largest* SISTERS *are sitting*)

Just to talk to Jesus
Oh, what a joy de-vine
Ah kin feel de lectric
Movin on de line,
All wired up by God de Father
For his lovin own,
Put a call to Jesus
On the Royal Telephone—

JACK (*over the singing*)

Here, where that Jew's-harp—

(*Finds it*)

Plung on it, Rudy, it cover you face up—

(*Tosses it to him.* RUDY *plays.* JACK *moves among them*)

Good luck—thank you—thank you—
see you soon—you too—don't worry—
Thank you, Momma Tiny—
Get well, darlin, try, please try—
Say you come an see me—good-bye, my momma,
Good-bye, my sweetheart—

(MRS. JEFFERSON *nods and sings right on, clapping to the beat, and with* GOLDIE *mopping his face,* CLARA *kicking and crying,* RUDY *twanging and* ALL THE REST *in full chorus,* JACK *puts on his cap and disappears with the* JAYS)

ALL

Angel operators
Waitin for you call,
Central up in heaven,
Take no time at all,
Ring, and God will answer
In his happy tone,
Put a call to Jesus
On the Royal Telephone.

CURTAIN ACT I

ACT 2

scene one

a chamber in the Home Office, London.

Some dozen chairs facing a large desk are arranged for the hearing about to take place. As the scene begins, SIX MEN *and* ONE WOMAN, *all middle-aged and soberly dressed, are seating themselves. From a door opposite,* EUBANKS, *assistant to the Undersecretary, enters chatting with* TREACHER, JACK's *solicitor. Enter* JACK, ELLIE, GOLDIE, TICK.

TREACHER
Ah, good morning—

EUBANKS
I'll go and fetch Sir William.

(Goes)

JACK
Mornin, evvybody . . . Mornin, Miz Kimball . . . How you today, Mac . . . ?

(THEY *stare straight ahead*)

Muss be de Wax Museum took a branch here.

TREACHER
Over there, please, Jack.

GOLDIE
And let Mr. Treacher
do the talking, understand?

103

TREACHER
Yes, thank you.

JACK (*to* ELLIE)
We straighten dis out, hon.

ELLIE
Well, I hope so.

JACK
Feelin kina edgy, huh.

ELLIE (*takes his hand*)
No.

TICK
Ah does.

EUBANKS (*entering*)
Sir William Griswold.

JACK (*to* ELLIE)
Hey, you breakin mah han!

(SIR WILLIAM *enters.* GOLDIE, TICK, *and the* WOMAN *stand up*)

SIR WILLIAM
Good morning—no, no need to rise, thank you.

(*Sits at desk*)

Yes . . . Now, then. Allegations have been made to us
concerning the possible undesirability
of an alien person's continued visit here.
We have of course our own book of rules on the subject,
and normally—

COATES
With due respect, Sir William,
I'm amazed that you find this necessary.

SIR WILLIAM
Mr.—?

COATES
Coates.

SIR WILLIAM (*to* EUBANKS)
Representing?

EUBANKS
British Vigilance Board.

COATES
Can you really be debating this?
A convicted criminal, a fugitive from justice—

TREACHER
My client's conviction was known to the authorities.
He was admitted at their discretion.

SIR WILLIAM
That is true, Mr. Coates.

COATES
And our discreet authorities are helpless to correct
their initial error, is that what you imply, sir?

SIR WILLIAM
I implied nothing, I'm sure.

COATES
Your official silence
indeed implies something! Like official license
for breaches of the peace, for moral deficiency
flaunted at the public—

JACK
Now wait—
Ah ain't flung no fish at no public!

COATES

I beg your—

TICK
Jack, you hush up—

SIR WILLIAM
Gentlemen, please—

MRS. KIMBALL (*the* WOMAN)
I'll tell them what you did do, you great flash nig-nog!

EUBANKS

Madam, really—

GOLDIE
Don't you talk like that, lady—

COATES

Mrs. Kimball here—

MRS. KIMBALL (*to* COATES)
Do I speak my piece now—?

EUBANKS

Mr. Coates has the—

COATES
No, go on, Mrs. Kimball.

MRS. KIMBALL
I rented him my luxury maisonette, your honor,
Ten Portman Square, and not many would rent to them,
believe you me, a black and white job to boot,
but I thought they at least was married, which they
wasn't,
and I thought she being white they'd be clean, which
they wasn't,
and I thought maybe them being lovebirds like they are
they'd settle down early nights—nothing of the kind!

Parties, champagne, nigger piano playing—
mind you, I like a bit of music, but I never,
all night, screaming up the stairwell. Oh, yes,
I'd see them through the door when I went to shut em
    up,
doing their dirty dances in there—**Turkey Trot
and all the rest of them colored steps!**

COATES

The damage to Mrs. Kimball's flat, Sir William,
was appraised at nearly four hundred pounds.

MRS. KIMBALL

Yes, that's right! Vases, Chippendale,
can't replace it neither—**and rubbish all over too,
the filthy ape! Undesirable!**

TREACHER
                The amount has been paid
in full, Sir William.

SIR WILLIAM
Who is next, Mr. Coates?

COATES
Inspector Wainwright.

EUBANKS
Metropolitan Police.

WAINWRIGHT (*reading from
notebook*)
November ninth. Charged with using
obscene language on Coventry Street. Fine, two pounds.
November fifteenth.
Charged with causing a crowd to collect. Fine, fifty
    shillings.
Fined a further five pounds for contempt of court.

SIR WILLIAM (*to* JACK)
Why the fine for contempt, may I ask.

JACK

Well, de judge he yell, Ah fine you fifty shillins!
So Ah says, Look, dat crowd's still collectin
so maybe you better take a hundred off me.

WAINWRIGHT

November twenty-fifth—

SIR WILLIAM (*to* COATES)

If the police offenses are all of this nature—

COATES

You may skip to January third, Wainwright.

WAINWRIGHT

January third.

Charged with assault on Mr. M. Bratby.

TREACHER

The charge has been dropped, Sir William.

COATES

Sir,

when a man trained in the use of his fists—

JACK

No, Ah juss shoved him—

(*To* BRATBY)

Whut you tell this man, Mac?

SIR WILLIAM

You are—?

BRATBY

M. Bratby.

EUBANKS

Olympia Sporting Club.

BRATBY

Jefferson came to us proposing that we match him.
We had been unwilling to associate ourselves with him—
we expressed this position—he became unruly—

COATES

Attacked you, you mean!

TREACHER

The affair has been settled, Mr. Jefferson's apology—

COATES

Yes, all the affairs are settled,
the popular press delightedly reports them,
and nightly in the music halls they are dealt with as a
  joke!
Is any of this desirable? This, when disruption
is the order of the day, with the ground we stand on
undermined by socialists, atheists, anarchists,
with anarchy not merely a word but a man
with a bomb in a public building—

SIR WILLIAM
                    Mr. Coates—

COATES

And you're amused, sir, when this lady refers to these
  dances
coming into vogue since this man's arrival here,
but read your Plato, Sir William, read your Plato—

SIR WILLIAM
                                I say—

COATES

"New modes of music herald upheavals of state," sir—

SIR WILLIAM

Now really, Mr. Coates, I have seen the Turkey Trot—

COATES

Let me remind you of the waltz, Sir William—

SIR WILLIAM

The waltz?

COATES

The first waltz, sir—

SIR WILLIAM

Are you asking me to dance—?

TREACHER

Sir William, may I venture—

JACK

No, Ah kin talk.

SIR WILLIAM

Yes, please. Go ahead.

JACK

Ah come over as a prizefighter, sir.
Figgered Ah could fight Billy Wells here or Jeannette,
an make me mah livin here the way Ah knows how.
But we coulden git no decent match fix up,
so Ah was juss gittin fat, and kickin up and fussin
   people.
Now, Ah guess Ah shouldn've,
cause whut Ah am, you know, cullud Ah mean,
some folks here think is a freak anyway,
but it took me some time gittin use to bein here,
an Ah'm sorry bout all these stories they brung in,
an whut Ah wanna say is, we like it here fine now,
and now Lord Londsale done set me up a match,
Ah'll git trainin an fightin an we won't have no mo
   rumpus.

SIR WILLIAM

Well, Mr. Coates, as I see this at the moment,

the American legalities are none of our concern,
the breaches of the peace you've cited are trivial,
the man's moral character deficient perhaps
by Queen Victoria's standards—**but she of course is gone
    now**—
and as to the palaver in the press and music halls
these are liberties we simply have to bear—
think of them as part of the White Man's Burden.
So unless Mr. Jefferson commits a crime of some sort—
which I hope none of you will tempt him to further—
I do not see—You have something to add?

COATES

I should like to correct Mr. Jefferson's assumption
that he does indeed have a match on, Sir William.

JACK

Whut you talkin bout, Ah sign up wid him dere—

(*Points to* BRATBY)

fightin Albert Lynch on March de eighteenth—

SIR WILLIAM

Is this relevant, Mr. Coates—

COATES
                Oh, I think so. Bratby?

BRATBY

Two weeks ago, at Lord Londsdale's persuasion,
we proposed this match, and Jefferson accepted.
It now appears, however, that the London County
    Council
refuses to issue a license for this fight.
And enquiries indicate this difficulty elsewhere.

TREACHER

Refused the license on what grounds?

COATES

Mr. Farlow?

FARLOW

I should say that Mr. Coates
has already expressed the Council's position.

JACK

Goldie, how the hell—

TICK

Sit easy there, baby—

COATES

This man entered England with the stated purpose
of pursuing his career as a pugilist. Now, what, sir,
are the grounds for his remaining in England
if this career of his does simply not exist here!

(JACK *stands,* ELLIE *holds him by the hand*)

SIR WILLIAM

Please sit down, sir.

(*To the others*)

I shall make no comment
on the principles or motives operating among you.
I shall only inform you that an alien is free
to change his means of livelihood, he may take up any—

JACK

OK. Les go.

TICK

De guy still—

JACK
Up!

(ELLIE *gets up and* TICK *gets up*)

SIR WILLIAM   (*to* JACK)
It is understood, I hope, that—

JACK
Come on, Goldie—

(*To* SIR WILLIAM)

Ah thank you fo you time, sir,
and stickin up fo me—

SIR WILLIAM
I'm really very sorry—

JACK
You scuse us now, please—

(*To* TREACHER)

See you, Mr. Treacher—

ELLIE
Jack—

COATES   (*to* TREACHER)
Your client will be leaving the country, I take it.

JACK
Yeah, man, you take it. It's all yours.

(BLACKOUT. *Boat whistle, train whistle, another boat
whistle, crowd, band playing.* LIGHTS UP *on*—)

scene two

a customs shed, Le Havre.

At one side, with the BAND, *a welcoming* CROWD: OFFI-
CIALS, PRESS, *etc., some waving small tricolors. At the
other side* TWO UNIFORMED INSPECTORS, *beyond them
a sign:* DOUANE. *Some* PORTERS *hurry past them,
wheeling trunks, and a* CHEER *goes up behind them.
Followed by his* ENTOURAGE, *greeting the* CROWD *with
hands clasped triumphantly over his head, appears*
KLOSSOWSKI, *a Polish heavyweight. The* PHOTOGRA-
PHERS' *flares commence, and continue through the
scene. The* BAND *stops playing as* KLOSSOWSKI *meets
the* OFFICIALS *and* PRESS, *shaking hands and embracing all around.*

OFFICIAL
Bienvenue encore à la France, Monsieur Klossowski!

CROWD
Bravo, Klossowski! Bienvenue! Bonne arrivée!

KLOSSOWSKI
Merci, merci, mes amis, mille mercis—

PRESSMAN 1
Alors, vous êtes prêt pour votre grand combat
avec le noir Jefferson?

KLOSSOWSKI
Oho, monsieur—je suis absolument—

PRESSMAN 1
Confiant?

KLOSSOWSKI

C'est ça! Con—fi—dent!
Je m'excuse que mon français est terrible—

CROWD

Mais non, mais non!

PRESSMAN 3

Mais vous n'êtes pas hésitant à faire la boxe
avec le champion du monde? Un petit peu?

KLOSSOWSKI

Hésitant! Ha, ha, ha!

CROWD
Bravo, Klossowski!

KLOSSOWSKI

Écoutez—
Je boxai à Buenos Aires avec Paco Flores!
            Zut! Zut! Zut! Trois rounds, je gagne!
Je boxai à Rio avec Pereira!
            Zut! Frappe! Deux rounds, je gagne!
Je boxai en Afrique avec un noir gigantesque là—
            Zut! Boom! Pas de conteste, messieurs!
Et cette Jefferson, qui c'est, qui c'est?
Oh, champion du monde, oui, lalala—
mais il n'a pas boxé pour longtemps!

   (*Miming it*)

Il boit le whiskey, il fume les cigares,
il est gros, il êtes lourde,
il vit comme un—un—

PRESSMAN 1
Cochon?

   (*Laughter*)

KLOSSOWSKI
C'est ça!

(*Laughter*)

Non, messieurs, c'est pas la vie du boxeur!

(*Mimes it all*)

Moi, je cours chaque jour trente kilomètres,
même à la bateau—oui!
Je saute à la corde: cent fois!
Je boxe l'ombre: une heure!
Petit sac, vingt minutes!
Des gymnastiques, quarante minutes, deux fois, matin
   et soir,
et bain chaud! Douche froid!
Forte massage après midi,
mange bien, dix heures sommeil—

(*Laughter*)

Vous pensez que j'éxagère?
Attendez le combat Jefferson—

(*Acts it out*)

et zut! Zut! Gauche à l'estomac!
Droite à la tête! Gauche encore!
Zut! Frappe! Boom! Dix!
Voilà—vous verrez!

(*Cheering,* THEY *hoist him on their shoulders, the*
BAND *strikes up, and he is borne off as* LIGHTS FADE:
new CROWD SOUND *gradually replacing cheering, an
arena* CROWD, *distant.* LIGHTS UP *on—*)

scene three

Jack's dressing room at the Vel d'Hiver arena, Paris.

JACK *is sitting on table.* TICK *taping his hands.* ELLIE. *A French* HANDLER *busy with towels, sponge, salts, etc.*

TICK

Keep breathin deep, champ, nice an slow now.

JACK

Ah knows howta breathe.

TICK

Gonna finish off dat Polack like a chicken dinner!

JACK

Hurry it up, huh.

TICK

Ain even gonna muss you wool up on him!

JACK

Don' talk like that fronna her.

ELLIE

Jack, don't be silly—

JACK

An when you start callin me "champ" anyway?

TICK

Hey, come on. See if that too tight now.

(GOLDIE *enters*)

ELLIE

Full house?

GOLDIE

Girlie, they're hangin from the rafters.

JACK

Water bottle, Tick. Wanna rinse.

GOLDIE

You OK?

JACK

Why you keep askin me?

GOLDIE

So what, so I'm askin!

JACK

You worried bout somethin? What you worrying bout!

TICK

Man, dat Polack sure in for it tonight.

GOLDIE

Tick, for chrissake—

TICK (*to* HANDLER)

Uh—hey, Jim, where that O bottle gone to?

HANDLER

Comment?

TICK

The O. You know, O?

HANDLER

Le—Ah—

TICK

No, the O—

HANDLER

La bouteille!

TICK

Mistah who?

JACK

Never mine—

HANDLER

Non?

TICK

Yeah, the O!

HANDLER

De l'eau!

(*Produces it*)

TICK

Attaboy! See? Juss be patient with em.

(*Gives it to* JACK, *who gargles and spits*)

JACK

Bad tase in there, thassall.

GOLDIE (*to* TICK)

Coupla more minutes.

TICK (*to* JACK)

Put em up, baby, we better warm up some.
Huh? OK?

JACK

Ah warm up inside there with the man.

TICK

Aw, be good now!

Ah ain't gonna get you winded—

ELLIE

Tick!

JACK

You don' haveta tell me what wind Ah ain't got.

TICK

No, man, Ah mean—

JACK

Ah know what shape is an when Ah ain in it.
Ah know when gettin in it's a waste a my good time too!
Ah don' gotta train to take no fith-rate geechee—

GOLDIE

Jack, who says different—

JACK

Thass who Ah fightin here, ain it!

GOLDIE

It's the best they got around here, Jack—

JACK

Hit him one an shovel up the money, right?
Jump in with the big gole belt, right?

TICK (*sings*)

**Niggers is evil
White folks too.
So glad Ah'm a Chinaman,
Don' know whut to do.**

(PROMOTER *enters*)

PROMOTER

If you please, messieurs.

ELLIE

I'll go in to my seat now.

JACK

Honey—

ELLIE (*kisses him*)

Good luck, darlin—

JACK

Do me a favor. Stay here.

ELLIE

Oh, Jack.

JACK

Nothin in there you wanna see.

PROMOTER

Come along, please, messieurs—

(*To* HANDLER)

vite, vite—

(*To* JACK)

But, oh, Monsieur Jefferson, the smile, the famous smile—
You will not deny to our public the smile!

JACK

No, Ah got it on me.

PROMOTER
Ha, ha, very good.

TICK

We won't be too long.

(THEY *leave.* ELLIE *sits. A few seconds go by and the* CROWD ROAR *increases in volume.* ELLIE *stands, wanders aimlessly, spies a newspaper, tries to read it,*

puts it down. Over the CROWD NOISES *the* ANNOUNCER'S
VOICE *is heard, incoherent.* ELLIE *folds a towel, a
jersey, sits again.* SMITTY *enters*)

SMITTY

Hi there, Miss Bachman.

ELLIE

Hello—

SMITTY

Smith, *Evening Mirror.* Smitty?

ELLIE

Oh, yes.

SMITTY

Mind if I—

ELLIE

Aren't you here for the fight?

SMITTY

Well, the boys'll dope me in.
He's at it again, that's the main thing.

ELLIE

Yes.

SMITTY

I've missed him, Old Jack. How is he, anyway?

ELLIE

Fine.

SMITTY

Sure is looking good! Oh, a little moody—

ELLIE

A little.

SMITTY
That'll pass, don't let it get you down.
Part of it's all this moving around.

ELLIE
Yes.

SMITTY
Once you're not, and settle in somewhere—

(*A* ROAR)

There they go! You know what I mean?

ELLIE
Yes.

SMITTY
Makes all the difference.

ELLIE
Probably.

SMITTY
Sure—
and how long can it be!

ELLIE
I don't know, really.

SMITTY
Bet you can't wait, huh? Either of you!

ELLIE
We talk about it.

SMITTY
Yeah, what a feeling—
like to have a little nest here, do you think?

ELLIE

We haven't made any—

(*A* ROAR. SHE *shivers*)

SMITTY
            Listen to em!
No idea?

(SHE *shakes her head*)

Christ, that must be hard on you now . . . hm?

(*No reply*)

Well, leave that all to Jack!
As long as you rest and keep your strength up—

(SHE *faces him. A* ROAR)

I've had four myself and let me tell you—

ELLIE

Go away, will you.

SMITTY
            Ah, be a sport,
when's it going to be?

ELLIE
            It's not. Go away.

SMITTY

I mean, you were looking so peaked the other day,
I had a hunch—

(*A* ROAR. SHE *turns away*)

            Say, don't get sore!
Look, the folks back home—

ELLIE
I told you: no!

SMITTY
I hate to let you down, folks!

(*A* ROAR)

ELLIE
Now, please—

(*A* ROAR)

SMITTY
Something else, maybe?
Wedding bells? Homesick? Hear from your family?

(*A* ROAR. SHE *covers her ears, shuddering*)

ELLIE
Oh, it's never—

SMITTY
Are you feeling OK, Miss Bachman?

ELLIE
Yes—

(*A* ROAR)

SMITTY
He's dishing it out, he's not getting it—

ELLIE
Please—

(*A* ROAR. SHE *bites her hand*)

SMITTY
You don't look too hot—Here, take a swallow—

(SHE *shakes her head. The* ROARING *is continuous now,* SMITTY *is nearly shouting*)

How long do you think you can take it, anyway,
living like this! It has to burn you out, Miss Bachman,
can't you see that? Burn you out!
You're not as tough as he is, you know, you can't just
go on—

(*The noise has turned to* ANGRY BOOS *and* CATCALLS; RUNNING FEET, *a* BELL CLANGING. SHOUTS *nearby:* "Sauvage! Assassin!" JACK, TICK, GOLDIE, *and the* PROMOTER *burst in, blood smears on* JACK's *gloves and chest. Sounds of* POLICE SCUFFLING *in the corridor*)

GOLDIE

God, why'd you keep—

PROMOTER

Quickly, please!

ELLIE

What happened—Jack—

JACK

He'll come out of it—

GOLDIE

Grab that bag—

JACK

It's all right, honey—

TICK

Yeah—just!

ELLIE

No—

PROMOTER

This way, please—

GOLDIE

Dress in the car, Jack—

PROMOTER

I beg of you!

JACK

Come on, honey. I'm sorry, I'm sorry.

(*Leads* HER *off*, LIGHTS *and* SHOUTS FADING. DARKNESS)

scene four

Pop Weaver's office, New York.

The darkened office suite of POP WEAVER, *promoter.
In the flickering light of the film* THEY *are watching
sit* POP, CAP'N DAN, *and* FRED, *formerly Brady's
manager.*

CAP'N DAN

How much you say he weighs, Fred?

FRED

Two thirty-seven. He's six foot five . . . watch it!
Mommer!

POP

Not bad, Cap'n Dan, eh?

FRED

Wait, here's Vancouver two weeks ago—hold on—
there's my boy! The one on the left.

CAP'N DAN

You couldn't exactly miss him, Fred.

FRED
Rushes straight in—there! I don't wanna brag,
but when that kid first—

(*The film breaks; only the beam continues*)

Ah, for crying out loud!

VOICE (*offstage*)
Won't take a minute.

FRED
So? Waddaya say!
If that's no White Hope I'm Queen Pocahontas.

POP
He's the right stuff, Dan. Maybe a little raw yet—

FRED
Fresh, fresh is what he is! Big, clean, strong,
a real farmboy! They're waiting on their knees
for something like him!

(*Silence.* THEY *stare at the blank screen*)

FRED (*calling out*)
How about it there!

CAP'N DAN
I don't think we need to see any more, Pop.

POP
Lights, please, Harry.

(*The room is lit*)

Well, you tell me, Dan.
You want me to promote it, I'm ready to promote it,
anytime, anywhere.

FRED (*to* CAP'N DAN)
Right!

POP
What do you think, Dan?

CAP'N DAN
I think he's a full-grown polar bear, myself.

FRED
Well, we have to send over somebody, don't we?
The papers are hollerin, all the old bull again—
Honest, it's gettin like Remember the Maine here!

CAP'N DAN
Oh, he fills the bill all right.
But say we do send him over, and the black boy
does it again, Fred. Then where are we.

POP
You won't ever have it on a plate, Dan, you know.

CAP'N DAN
Pop, Fred. Let me tell you a secret.
The next White Hope is the one who gets the belt back.
Not means to, or almost does, or gets half-killed trying:
he takes it, he finishes right on his feet, with a big
horizontal nigger down for good there.

POP
What do you mean, Dan? Is it yes or no.

CAP'N DAN
I'd like you to meet a friend of mine, Pop.

(*Calls*)

Mr. Dixon there yet?

VOICE (*offstage*)
Yeah!

CAP'N DAN
Come on in.

(*Enter* DIXON)

Pop Weaver. Fred.

POP
Have a chair, Mr. Dixon.

DIXON (*sits*)
Thanks.

(*To* CAP'N DAN)

All right?

CAP'N DAN
Oh, we're hopeful, I think.

(THEY *laugh*)

Dixon here is with the Bureau in Washington.
Like you might expect, they have Mr. Jefferson
on their minds, too. I've been down there,
we've had some ideas—you explain it to them, son.

DIXON
When a man beats us out like this, we—the law, that is—
suffer in prestige, and that's pretty serious.
How people regard the law is part of its effectiveness,
it can't afford to look foolish, and this applies
especially now to our Negro population.
I don't mean just the ones who always flout the law,
and seeing their hero doing it in style
act up more than usual—those are police concerns, not
    ours.
But though you may not be aware of it yet,
a very large, very black migration is in progress.

They're coming from the fields down there and filling
  up the slums,
trouble's starting in Europe, and our mills and factories
have work for them now. And I'm talking of hundreds
of thousands, maybe millions soon—
millions of ignorant Negroes, rapidly massing together,
their leanings, their mood, their outlook, suddenly
no longer regulated by the little places they come from—
situations have arisen already.
We cannot allow the image of this man
to go on impressing and exciting these people.

POP

I'm only a sports promoter, Mr. Dixon.

CAP'N DAN

He read the writing on the door, Pop. Go on.

DIXON

If this position he enjoys were to be lost,
through the outcome of his next engagement, let's say,
the effect of this would be so much in our interest
that we would be disposed to reconsider his sentence.

POP

You'd make it worth his while not to win the fight, you
  mean.

DIXON

I think I've said what I mean, Mr. Weaver.

CAP'N DAN (*to* DIXON)

What's the furthest you can go.

DIXON

We'd reduce it to a year, of which he'd serve six months,
preferred treatment, best facilities, etcetera.
We're willing to make this as attractive as possible.

FRED

I say my kid can beat him fair and square!

POP

Don't ride it, Fred.

FRED

Look, if you won't promote it,
I'll hop on a boat with him and find someone who will!

CAP'N DAN

You don't want to do that, Fred.

FRED

What am I, a—

CAP'N DAN

Fred. I'm tellin you as a friend.

FRED

I just don't like it.

POP

It goes against me too, Dan.

CAP'N DAN

And against me too!
I don't have to make anybody no speech here
about how good I feel working something crooked!
None of us like it—we wouldn't be the men we are
if we did, or be where we are! I know it's lousy!
But we got a situation here needs a little bending,
the man's tried to tell you how serious it is,
they're bending with it, I'm bending with it,
who are you to sit there and say it goes against you,
or you either, on your pedestal here!

POP

What about the champ, though, Dan?

FRED

He'll never buy it!
Or my kid either, he's straight outa Sunday school,
he's—

CAP'N DAN

Shut up, Fred—
nobody has to tell your kid a thing!
And Jack, well, after that last one,
nobody there'll fight him any more,
he's down to giving exhibitions, peanuts—

POP

But serving six months, Dan—

CAP'N DAN

It can't be much worse
than killing the six months. And he'll step out a free
man—
all that fight money! See all his pals!
Besides, his ole mammy ain't been too good,
he'll want to see her before she goes.
Sure he'll take it.

POP

Dan, why not ask Weiler
or Michel to set it up, someone on the spot there?

CAP'N DAN

I'm asking you, Pop.

(*Pause*)

POP (*to* DIXON)
You can't put that deal
in writing, can you, mister?

DIXON
Sorry, Pop. I wasn't even here.

(*Pause*)

POP

What the hell, Fred.
We'll balance it out on the one after this.
Everything back on the gold standard, right?

FRED

OK, OK.

DIXON (*rising*)
Well, thank you, gentlemen—

(THEY *all rise*)

CAP'N DAN

And we thank you!

POP
I wouldn't count on
results straight off, though.

DIXON
Oh, I think the country
can hold up a little while.

(THEY *laugh*, DIXON *waves them silent*)

Excuse me—
You seem to be indignant, sir. Yes, I heard you.
We have that all the time from people like you,
that old Machiavelli crap. Look into it further, sir.
But not in here, or at home. Give it some thought
next time you're alone on the streets late at night.

(*To* CAP'N DAN)

I'll be in touch with you.

(LIGHTS FADE. BLACKOUT. MUSIC: *German street band,
distant.* LIGHTS UP *on*—)

scene five.

a sidewalk café, Berlin.

JACK, TICK, *four drunken* GERMAN OFFICERS *with them.*
JACK *Indian-wrestling the largest,* OFFICER 4, *on the
stein-covered table, as the other three encourage
their comrade.*

OFFICER 1

Jetzt!

OFFICER 2

Kraft, Hans—

OFFICER 3

Ringe!

OFFICER 4

Kann nicht!

OFFICER 1

Nein!

OFFICER 4

Himmelsgott!

OFFICER 2

Ja!

(JACK *begins to bear his arm down*)

OFFICER 3

Aber, Hans—

OFFICER 1

Nein!

OFFICER 4
Mutter!

OFFICER 2
Halt—

OFFICER 1
Nein—

OFFICER 3
Nein, nein—

ALL
A-a-a-h!

OFFICER 1
Wunderbar! **Herrlich!** Mein herr, you are the triumph!

JACK
Well, thanks for stoppin roun, boys—

OFFICER 2
Wir müssen die Fahne vom Regiment präsentieren!

OFFICER 1
He says we must present to you the flag of our regiment!

JACK
Oh, cain't take that, ahma Mercan citizen—

TICK
You buy some tickets fo de show, dassall—

OFFICER 4 (*offering his arm*)
Bitte—again, please—

JACK
Tomorrow, buddy, you done wore me out.

(ALL OFFICERS *laugh*)

TICK
We see you all tomorrow, huh?

OFFICER 1 (*picking up stein*)
Kameradschaft!

(*The* OTHERS *follow suit*)

JACK (*standing*)
Camera shaft, OK.

TICK
Lawd, the drinkin sure hard on the feet here.

OFFICER 4
Wir müssen ihm etwas geben!

ALL
Ja! Ja!

OFFICER 1
Mein herr, we go provide for you the suitable memento.

JACK
Great, be lookin out for ya.

TICK
Weenersane, weenersane.

ALL OFFICERS (*leaving*)
Hop, hop, hop, hop . . .

JACK (*yawning and stretching*)
O mah bones, whut you after.

TICK
Wanna go back to the hotel?

JACK (*sits*)
Naw. Nothin doin there. You ready fo anuther?

TICK

Ah better pass.

(*Sips*)

Wonder how they make it brew up so heavy.
You think they mix a egg in or whut?

JACK

Beats me, man. Puttin me to sleep, though.

TICK

Well, thass whut they does after lunch here, right?

JACK

No, man, that were someplace else.

(ELLIE *enters with* RAGOSY, *an impresario*)

RAGOSY

Ah, Meester Jafferson—

JACK

Whut you bring him for—?

RAGOSY

Such delights again to see you—

JACK

Now ain Ah tole you, mistah—

RAGOSY

Ragosy, excuse—

(*Gives card*)

ELLIE

He just tagged along, Jack—

RAGOSY

I am patient rewarded!

TICK

Which one wuz he?

JACK

Huh ... lemme think now ...
You ain't the one wanted me to team up with a circus—

RAGOSY

Please?

JACK

An it wuzn't you pushin me to start a restrunt with
him—

RAGOSY

No, no—

JACK

Or the artiss guy gonna hire me an do me in black
cement?

RAGOSY

But you recall Ragosy!

TICK

Man, he that Hungrarian!

JACK

Oh yeah, thassright—

(WAITER *enters*)

RAGOSY

Please, not speak additional word,
I supply first champagne—

(*To* WAITER)

                              Abräumen, bitte!

(*To* JACK)

Wait, not to trust here, I consult myself—sit!

(*Goes in*)

JACK (*to* ELLIE)

Why dinya sen him up ta Goldie, Goldie brush him!

ELLIE

He wasn't there, he had to go out.

TICK

Oh yeah? Something movin?

ELLIE

Just meeting that reporter.

JACK

Smitty?

ELLIE

Yes, he rang up.

JACK

Whut he doin here?

TICK

Must be he onna job an he sayin hello.

JACK

Nothin goin on here.

TICK

You ain't the only item in the paper, bighead.

RAGOSY (*reentering with champagne;* WAITER *sets glasses*)

See, from my own hands! I take it the privilege—
Champion, lovely friends—

TICK
> Ready wid de pumps, men.

RAGOSY
Oh, Meester Jafferson!
It pains in my heart these nights attending you.
I count there the people and I make totality:
one-quarter business! you do not divert!

JACK
Mebbe Ah oughta wear a bone through mah nose.

RAGOSY
No, no!
For the true fisticuff with bleedings they come,
but now you are not doing, you must look otherwise.
I implore again myself, let Ragosy be devising
the spectacle to you—Song! Dancing! **Sentiment!**
The name is on you still like a diamond, my friend,
only let make necessary light and then, then—

JACK (*leaping up: buck
and wing*)
> **Out in San Francisco where de weather's fair**
> **Dey have a dance out dere—**

RAGOSY
Ah, aha—

JACK
> **Dey call the Grizzly Bear,†**
> **All your other lovin' dances don't compare—**

ELLIE
Jack, please stop it.

JACK
What?

ELLIE
Can't you just tell him no and—

JACK

Ah tell him whut Ah wants to, hon—

ELLIE

Jack, we're in the street—

JACK

An where Ah wants to an how, hear?

TICK

Baby, all she sayin—

JACK

Who ass you!

(*To* ELLIE)

Talk to me bout streets.
If you so goddam tetchy bout people lookin
you ain't even oughta be here!

ELLIE

I don't like them looking when you're this way—

JACK

No? Well, me neither! But Ah's stuck widdit
an you ain't, so any time you wanna—where you goin!

RAGOSY (*rising*)

Oh, Madam, I sincerely—

JACK (*to* ELLIE)

Git you ass back on there! Man bought champagne—

RAGOSY

Please, Meester Jafferson—

JACK

You siddown too!

(RAGOSY *does*)

ELLIE

I'll be in the room.

JACK

Yeah, then you say you sicka waitin roun hotels!

ELLIE

I never said that.

JACK

You givin out you misery so hard you don' haveta!
You juss don' like nothin no more!

ELLIE

I won't even answer you—

JACK
Dassit, give it out!

ELLIE

What do you want, Jack!

JACK
Don' like nothin!

ELLIE (*going*)

Excuse me, please—

JACK
You siddown here, girl—

TICK

Let her go, man, she got the Fear again—

JACK (*calling after her*)
ELLIE!

TICK (*following*)

Ah walk her on back—

(NOISE *of rhythmical clanging and shouting*)

JACK

Tell that Goldie Ah wants him, hear!

TICK (*looking in direction
of noise*)

Say—

JACK

Git!

(*Holds ears*)

Oh, them heavy-foot bastuds.

TICK (*going*)

He turnin meaner than a red hyena.

JACK (*toasting* RAGOSY)

Happy days, mistah—

RAGOSY

Prosit, prosit, and I eagerly to hope we—

(RAGOSY *slips off as the* FOUR OFFICERS *gaily return:
one is beating on dustbin lid with a chair leg, two of
the others frog-march between them a very black
young* NEGRO, *who struggles violently*)

NEGRO

Lassen mir! Lassen mir absteigen!

JACK

Hey—

OFFICER 1

So, we bring you as we promise—halt!

OFFICER 4

Einen Schwarzen Kameraden—

(Laughing, THEY *dump* NEGRO. JACK *helps him up)*

JACK

Here, lemme duss you off—

OFFICER 2

Is suitable, nein?

NEGRO

Mutig Soldaten spielen wie Kinder!

(Jeers and laughter)

JACK

Don' rile em, man—

NEGRO

Again, bitte?

JACK

Whut—where the hell you from, anyway?

OFFICER 1

Where! He must ask!

(Gales of laughter)

NEGRO

Afrika.

OFFICER 2

Boomboomboom!

OFFICER 4

Crucrucru!

OFFICER 3

Authentick, ja!

JACK

Oh, Jesus.

OFFICER 1
Here, you observe?

(Points to scars on NEGRO's *face.* JACK *gasps. More laughter)*

NEGRO
Ja. Iss tribe mark.

OFFICER 2
Walawalawala!

NEGRO
Here iss custom more large.

(Makes gesture of dueling scar. OFFICER 4 *goes for him)*

OFFICER 4
Scheissfarbiger Hund—

OFFICER 2 *(as other* OFFICERS *tussle with* OFFICER 4, *restraining him)*
Nein, Hans, nein—

JACK
Go siddown there, Jim—

NEGRO
Please?

JACK *(pushing him toward table)*
Move—

(Going to struggling OFFICERS)*

Well, much obliged, fellahs, thass zackly what Ah wanted—

(OFFICER 4 *breaks away,* JACK *catches him by arm*)

Hey, Hands, you know this one?

　(*Stands with him toe to toe*)

> OFFICERS 1, 2, 3
> Ah!

> OFFICER 2

Wirf ihn!

> OFFICER 3

Jetzt! Jetzt!

> OFFICER 1

Nun, Hans—

　(JACK *pulls him off balance*)

> **ALL OFFICERS**

Bravo!

> OFFICER 2
> **Der schaffts immer!**

> OFFICER 4　(*to* WAITER)

Herr Ober, Bier für uns alle!

> JACK
> No, Hands—

　(*Drawing them away*)

Bess leave us darkies get quainted . . . you know, chomp a few bananas an all—

> OFFICERS 3 *and* 4　(*laughing*)

Er muss eine Banane essen! Ja!

OFFICER 2

He pleases you, the new Kamerad, Herr Boxer!

JACK (*drawing them further*)

Man, Ah'm happy as a cow with six tits.

(*Shrieks of laughter.* THEY *go.* JACK *waves after them*)

Weenersane! Donker!

(*Returning*)

Wish they'd start a war up and keep them boys busy.

NEGRO (*standing at table*)

You forgiff I am employed in siss, please.

JACK

Thass awright, chief. Needed some ex'cise anyway.

NEGRO

I am nutt chiff. I am son from ser chiff.

JACK

Oh, yeah? Well, take a pew here with the fiel'-nigger's boy.

(THEY *sit,* JACK *pours*)

NEGRO

You are ser Boxer, ja?

JACK

Thass me. When Ah workin at it.

NEGRO

From Amerika kommen.

JACK

Yeah, kommen and goin. You never been there, Ah guess.

NEGRO

Nein. I haff nutt zere ser purpose. Iss gutt?

JACK

Sometimes. Ain been there a while myself.

NEGRO

You learn zere gutt make ser laughink.

JACK

Oh, thanks.

NEGRO

Please, iss nutt uffenz. Must I learn also, I sink.

JACK (*laughs*)

Seem like you leff it kina late.

NEGRO

Iss better, nein?

JACK

Yeah, mebbe so . . . Well, here's to us fish outa water.

(THEY *drink*)

NEGRO

Away much long iss to hurt now. You.

JACK

Might say that.

NEGRO

I am feeling. I haff in Europe sree year so.

JACK

Lawd. Lit out for good, huh?

NEGRO

Please?

JACK

Vamoose fum de ole country, Africa.

NEGRO

Ah! You sink I go for nutt be zere,
nein, nein. I go so I komm zere back.

JACK

How zat?

NEGRO

Mit more knowings.

JACK

Oh! Ah gotcha.

NEGRO

Student.

JACK

Yeah. Nevah touch it myself.

NEGRO

I do nutt tell to giff shame inn.

JACK

Huh? No, Ah'm with you, man.
What all you studyin?

NEGRO

Ser Law and ser Finanz and ser Chemikals-mining.

JACK

My, my, my.

NEGRO

Ja, makes ser headache!

(JACK *laughs with him*)

JACK

Better go warn de chief bout dis one!

NEGRO

Please? You haff choke mit ser fazzer?

JACK

Naw . . .

But Ah thought Mistah White running things down
   there.

NEGRO

Now, ja.

JACK

They gonna letya help, huh?

NEGRO

So, I vatch.

JACK

They ain leavin go, man. No place.

NEGRO

Zumorrow, nein.

JACK

Nex Wensdy nine neither.

NEGRO

Sey make here ser war soon, ja?

JACK

So?

NEGRO

Iss like drunken peoples,
Sree mann, fife mann, hitting one ozzer—you haff see,
   Boxer?
All ser teess mit bloot, outspitten!

Up all ser eatings, POUAH, POUAH!
Sey make so enough ser war,
plack mann fly out from ser mouss. I sink.

JACK *(takes it in, then
lifts his glass)*
Here's to you an me an de "How Long Blues."

NEGRO

Please?

JACK

Drink up.

NEGRO

Ah, Boxer. Goes like you Pessimismus
in Amerika all plack mann, I am fearing.

JACK

Well, don't go by me, buddy.

NEGRO

Ach, aber ja.
Goes plack Champion so, goes kleine plack mann so!
Logik, ncin?

JACK
He a bitch, ain he.

NEGRO

Bad, stronk peoples to be so.

JACK

Oh, man, we strong on cryin there, thassall.

NEGRO

Nein, was slafe. Slafe nutt stronk, he die.
Cry iss from ser life inn.

JACK

Well, it sure the wrong kina strong to git leff with
when you ain slavin no more.

NEGRO

You komm gutt out. You.

JACK

Outa where.

NEGRO

Ser slafe. I see.

JACK

Ah dunno. Juss went the whole hog, man.

NEGRO

Please?

JACK

Shoot it all. You know: jump.

NEGRO
            Ja, exakt.

(*Points at him*)

Ser bekinnink-man.

JACK

Naw, Ah ain tried ta start nothin.

(NEGRO *bursts out laughing*)

What so funny bout dat?

NEGRO (*rocking with laughter*)
Oh, Boxer, Boxer, Boxer,
ven I am to chumping in Afrika,
I hope so much nossing vill I make!

(GOLDIE *bursts in*)

GOLDIE

Jack! All over town I—oh, you busy?

(NEGRO *rises*)

JACK

Don' run off, man—

GOLDIE

Gotta talk to ya, Jack.

NEGRO

So, I go.

(JACK *rises.* NEGRO *removes object from shirt*)

Please, you take?

JACK

Oh, hey,—

NEGRO

Please. My fazzer giff.

JACK   (*hesitates, then takes it*)

Wish you all the luck in the worl, man, thanks.

NEGRO

Also you. You keep mit, ja?

JACK

Sure. Zat what it's for? Luck?

NEGRO

Nein. For hurt from spirits.

JACK

Yeah.

NEGRO

Gootbye, Boxer.

(NEGRO *bows and goes*)

JACK

OK, I'm listenin.

GOLDIE

Well . . . we got a match.

JACK

How much Ah get for losin it?

GOLDIE

Huh?

JACK

Yeah, Ah'm listenin.

GOLDIE

How the hell does he know!

JACK

Mah witch-doctor tole me.

GOLDIE

Look! Lemme first explain what Smitty—

JACK

Boss, Ah know whut Smitty.
They askin fo a straight fight, they ain't sendin Smitty—

GOLDIE

Whattaya gettin sore, the guy calls me up—

JACK

Nobody sore. How much it worth?

GOLDIE

Fred's got this kid, see—

JACK

Now, boss, you ain't hearin good.

GOLDIE

Eighty-twenty split. A hundred G's guarantee.

JACK

Mm, boy!

Pretty nice fo plain ole layin down, huh!

GOLDIE

And they'll cut the rap to six months for ya.

JACK

Well!

See all folks kin do when evvybody pitch in?

GOLDIE

Jackie, I don't blame you for—

JACK

Any special roun they like me to dive in?

GOLDIE

He says we can work all that out.

JACK

Uh huh. An whut you say?

GOLDIE

I said it stinks but I'll let him know later.

JACK (*pointing to champagne*)

Right.

Sen him a bottle a this, an tell him
suck it through a straw.

GOLDIE

No thinkin it over.

JACK

How long you my manager?

GOLDIE

Five-six years.

JACK

Then why you gotta ask?

GOLDIE

Why? Cause I gotta eat, that's why!
What am I managin here, for God's sake!
What else you got in fronta you—

JACK

Don't try an sell me, boss.

GOLDIE

Big shot! Send him champagne! On what?
The fights you have with your girl, maybe?
On a ten percent like this my enemies should live!

JACK

Ah know it, man. Time to fine fresh meat.

GOLDIE

Well, what the hell you need me for, anyway!

JACK

Yeah, been thinkin bout that—

(*The* FOUR OFFICERS *charge in.* THEY *carry a rope*)

OFFICER 4 (*to* WAITER)
Herr Ober, Bier für uns alle!

GOLDIE

Jack, let's go talk to him, they're gonna keep after you,
you're getting sick here—

JACK
No, you call it right—

OFFICER 1 (*giving* JACK *one end*)
We make now to pull, Boxer?

JACK
Yeah, why not—

GOLDIE
Listen—

OFFICER 3 (*as* OFFICERS *take
other end*)
Erst, Hans!

JACK
There's no hard feelins, boss—

OFFICER 4 (*as* THEY *all line up*)
Nun gewinnen wir!

GOLDIE
Jack—

JACK
Take all you need to get home on—

OFFICER 1
Prepared, mein herr?

JACK (*getting a grip*)
Anytime!

(*Tug of war:* JACK *holds*)

GOLDIE
Oh, Jackie, oh, look at what you're doin—

JACK (*giving ground*)

It . . . ain't . . . good . . . but . . . it's . . . the . . .
bess . . . Ah . . . can . . .

OFFICERS (*pulling him out
as* LIGHTS FADE)

Ho-ya! Ho-ya! Ho-ya! Ho-ya!

(BLACKOUT. *Cymbal crash, followed by a tinny render-
ing of "Chiri-biri-bin" as* LIGHTS UP *on*—)

scene six

Cabaret Ragosy, Budapest.

Small stage of a cabaret, audience unseen. A JUG-
GLER *in tights, working in time to the waltz, is
finishing his turn.* LOUD APPLAUSE *as* HE *takes his
bow;* RAGOSY, *now in evening dress and beaming,
joins him on the stage and boosts the applause. Exit
the* JUGGLER. RAGOSY *holds up his hand for silence.*

RAGOSY

És most, Hölgyeim es Uraim,
amire mindanyian vártak! Bemutatom
a Rágosy Kabaré föattrakcióját,
Amerikai klasszikust
"Uncle Thomas Kunyhóját."

(*The saxophone begins playing "My Old Kentucky
Home," and the* LIGHTING *becomes very roseate, as*
TWO STAGEHANDS *position a papier-mâché weeping
willow and a patch of grass.* RAGOSY *continues accord-
ingly, describing the scene*)

A jelenet a Mississippi . . . partjan jatszodik le . . .
sek sek . . .
Uncle Thomas és a little Éva élvezték a napkeltét . . .

(*Winding up to bring them on*)

Tehát bemutatjuk a világbajnokot Jack Jeffersont,
elbübölö feleségével és néger barátjával!

(*Spatter of applause.* ELLIE *comes on as Little Eva,
golden curls, etc.* JACK *follows her as Uncle Tom,
shabby, gray wig, etc.* SHE *sits under "tree"*)

ELLIE

Here, Uncle Tom, do come and sit beside me.

JACK

Deed Ah will, Miss Eva. On dis lubly ole grassy bank.

ELLIE

See how beautiful the clouds are, Tom. And the water
too.

JACK

An you right widdem, Miss Eva, you de byootifluss of all.

ELLIE

But, friend, why do you seem sad this evening?

JACK

Oh, Miss Eva, you and de Massah so kine ter Ole Tom
he juss gotta cry bout it now and den.

ELLIE

Yes. We are happy here.

JACK

It like a plantation fum de Good Book, yessum.
You de brightest lil sperrit Ah evah seed, Miss Eva.

ELLIE

Oh, Tom, sing about the Spirits Bright, would you?

JACK

Juss gittin set to.

(*Piano gives him a chord and accompanies. Sings.*)

Ah sees a ban uh Sperrits Bright
Dat tase de glo-ries dere—

(*Mock* GROAN *from the audience*)

Dey are all robed in spotliss white
An wavin palm dey bear.
Ef Ah had wings—

(*Another mock* GROAN, *a* TITTER, *a* VOICE *saying "kö-vetkező"*; JACK *stops, the piano stops. A moment of uncertainty*)

ELLIE

Oh, but look who has come to make us lively, Tom!

(*Enter* TICK *as Topsy, grinning and prancing*)

TICK

Hee, hee, hee!

ELLIE

Dear me, Topsy, why do you behave so!

TICK

Speck cause Ah jes plain ole wicked, Miss Eva!

JACK

What dis lil black imp done now?

TICK

Hee, hee, hee!

ELLIE

How old are you, Topsy?

TICK

Ah dunno, missy.

ELLIE

Don't you know how old you are? Who was your mother?

TICK

Ah dunno, missy. Nevah had no mother.

ELLIE

What do you mean? Where were you born?

TICK

Ah dunno, missy. Nevah wuz bo'n.

ELLIE

But Topsy, think a moment. Someone must have made you!

TICK

Nobody's Ah knows on, missy. Ah specks Ah jes growed!

ELLIE

Oh, Topsy—

TICK

Hee, hee, hee!

JACK

Awright, you shifless heathen, give us a breakdown an git back to yo stinks—

(*Piano and drums, assisted by* ELLIE, *who produces a tambourine, and* JACK, *a Jew's harp.* TICK *sings*)

TICK

I always think I'm up in Heaven*
When I'm down in Dixieland,
I've got an angel of a Mammy,
Out in Alabamy,

Of the good old fashioned brand;
She taught me that it's wrong,
To stay up all night long;
Go to sleep my baby,
That's Mammy's little fav'rite song.

(*Dances through the next chorus,* JACK *joining him,*
ELLIE *continuing on the tambourine. The audience
seems to like this better, but as* TICK, *breathless, resumes singing, they again grow more and more rest-
less*)

Everybody loves somebody
Down in dear old Dixieland,
The pretty flowers in the garden,
Keep their heads a noddin,
When you walk by hand in hand;
The gals down there are very plain—

(RAGOSY *tries to quiet audience*)

And every other lane's a lovers lane,
That's why—

(RAGOSY *pulls* TICK *from the stage, motioning to* JACK
and ELLIE *to continue.* ELLIE *reclines in a moribund
attitude against the tree as the saxophone com-
mences with "Old Black Joe"*)

JACK
Is you feelin . . . weakish agin, Miss Eva?

ELLIE
Yes. There is something I must tell you, Uncle Tom.

(*Protest from the audience*)

JACK
It cain't be, Miss Eva, not yit—

ELLIE

Do not be gloomy! Look, those clouds,
they are like great gates of pearl now.

(*More protests*)

JACK

No, Miss Eva, no—

ELLIE

And I can see beyond them . . . far, far off . . .

VOICE

Gyorsan, gyorsan!

JACK (*kneeling*)

Oh, Ah knows we cain't speck ta keep ya here wid us—

VOICE

Milyen unalmas!

ELLIE

Yes, I am going to a better country—

VOICE

A következö!

(*Laugh*)

ELLIE

And I am going there before long, Uncle Tom . . .

(*Groan*)

VOICES

Rémes! Rettentes!

JACK

Well, ef de Lawd needya back, Miss Eva—

VOICE

Hozd vissza a néger barátodat—!

JACK

Ah be hunkydory here—

VOICES

Rémes! Rémes!

(*A slow* HANDCLAP *starts in the audience, quickly building up with* FOOT-STAMPING *and* BOTTLE-KNOCK-ING)

ELLIE

Oh, dear Tom . . . take a tress of my . . .

VOICES

Borzasztó! Nevetséges!

(JACK *rises slowly, looks out at them*)

ELLIE

Take a tress of my golden hair . . . to . . . to . . .

(SHE *stops as the* NOISE *gets louder.* RAGOSY *appears at the side of the stage, trying to quiet them again, but they grow more angry at this*)

VOICES

Takaradjanak el!
Takaradjanak el!
Fogják meg!

(RAGOSY *tries to speak but cannot be heard;* ELLIE *runs from the stage.* JACK *pulls the Uncle Tom wig off and stands immobile, expressionless.* RAGOSY, *frightened, signals desperately—for* JACK *to get off-stage, for the saxophonist to stop playing, for the electrician to cut the lights . . . the saxophone desists, and after a few attempts the electrician seems*

to find the right switch . . . as the LIGHTS DIM OUT
on JACK *the* NOISE *reaches a crescendo, then is cut off
sharply in the* BLACKOUT *as, suddenly, at the extreme
opposite end of the real stage,* MRS. BACHMAN *appears,
white, pained, and haggard.* SHE *looks around at the
real audience, then speaks*)

MRS. BACHMAN

I know what most of you watching this believe in,
or think you believe in, or try to believe in.
But I know something else too, I know what Black
        means,
and not just to me because of my daughter,
to everyone in here. All of us know,
though it might take some of you a daughter you've
        cared for
to make you say it, what it means, yes, means,
what it is to you truthfully—BLACKNESS!—there, feel
        it,
what it sets off in your heart, in the memories and words
and shapes you think with, the dark to be afraid of,
pitch black, black as dirt, the black hole and the black
        pit,
what's burned or stained or cursed or hideous,
poison and spite and the waste from your body
and the horrors crawling up into your mind—
I hate what I'm saying! As much as you do!
I hate that it's so, I wish to God it weren't!
And if it was God who intended it so,
and still willed that color on a race of human beings,
and brought us face to face here,
how He must hate all of us! Go on imagining
that time and justice can change it in you now,
or that when it disappears in the singing of songs
it's being destroyed. Tell yourselves it's only
one more wrong to be righted, and that I'm a half-mad
        woman,
oh, making far too much of it. Wait until it is
your every other thought, like it is theirs, like it is mine.
Wait until it touches your own flesh and blood.

(As SHE *slowly walks off, the* LIGHTS *on her fading, a distant* RUMBLE *of artillery fire is heard, which continues throughout the next scene—)*

scene seven

railway station, Belgrade.

JACK *and* ELLIE *standing bedraggled in wet raincoats. Suitcases. Pools of light. Station empty.*

TICK *(entering)*
Nothin, man. Maybe one pullin out tonight.

JACK
Anybody know whut goin on dere?

TICK
Porter say dey just practicin.

JACK
Yeah.

ELLIE
What will we do, Jack?

JACK
I dunno yet.

ELLIE
Do you think we should—

JACK
Ah said Ah dunno yet!

ELLIE

All right, I heard you.

JACK

Play cards or somethin wid her, willya?

SMITTY *(offstage)*
Jack!

(Entering from a distance, catching his breath)

God, I'm glad I caught you . . .

JACK
Lay offa me, man.

SMITTY

It's sort of an emergency, Jack . . . back home.

(Takes out telegram)

Your mother's very low.

JACK *(snatching it from him)*
Gimme dat.

(Reads it. Holds onto it throughout scene)

SMITTY

I'm sorry about this, feller.

JACK
Yeah. Thanks.

SMITTY

Maybe we could work something out for you, Jack.
To go straight over now and then do the rest of it.
I know you want to be there.

(Pause)

You might just make it, Jack.
I've hired a car and I fixed up your passage from—

JACK (*to himself*)
Button comin loose here.

ELLIE
Yes?

(*Pause*)

SMITTY
Christ, deal or no deal,
it's worth a try, isn't it? Even just to let her
feel you're on your way, she'd be—

JACK
Thanks for comin roun, man.

SMITTY
You can't stay over here now, anyway. Jack!
It's finished here. You know that. Where do you go?

JACK
Don' wan none today, man.

SMITTY
All right, don't get sore—

I really thought—

JACK
Ah seeya sometime.

(*Pause*)

SMITTY
OK . .

(*Turns to go, stops*)

What the hell is it for, though, all this.
I mean, you're not a Boy Scout. What the hell is it, Jack.
Keeping the belt a little bit longer? Staying champ
a little while longer? I can't make you out.

JACK

Champ don' mean piss-all ta me, man.
Ah bin it, all dat champ jive bin beat clear outa me.
Dat belt a yours juss hardware, woulden even hole mah
    pants up.
But Ah'm stuck widdit, see, a hunk of junky hardware,
but it don' let go, it turnin green on me,
but it still ain lettin go, Ah'm stuck as bad widdit
as you all stuck wid needin it offa me—
shake it loose, man! Knock me fo ten and take it,
    understan?
Ah be much oblige!

SMITTY

                Look, you know we'd rather
have it straight—

JACK

                Oh, ya would, huh.

SMITTY

                                Sure,
and, Jack, if you weren't so damned good—

JACK (grabbing him)

Hunnerd million people ovah dere, ain'tya?

SMITTY

                                        Yes, but—

JACK

Picked out de bess Hope ya got dere, ain'tya—?

TICK

Jack—

JACK
Ah wants a match widdim—

SMITTY
It's our way or nothing, feller—

JACK
Ah said a match widdim!
An if you don' wanna gimme one, Ah gonna makeya,
same's Ah done before, see—

(*Releasing him*)

Ah gonna make em!
Gonna take mah funky suitcase an mah three-four hundred dollahs,
an git mahself ta Mexico, howya like dat, man,
right up nex ta ya, gonna sit on dat line dere
an wave you crummy belt atya an sing out
Here Ah is—

SMITTY
It's not going to work, Jack—

JACK
Dassall Ah got worth tryin now—

(*Crumpling the telegram*)

dis ain't, dis ain't,
Ah know dis pass trying, Ah—

TICK
Easy—

ELLIE
Jack, I'm so sorry—

JACK
Took too much outa her, Ah guess, she musta—
musta juss—

(*Strikes himself a blow on the forehead, staggers*)

ELLIE

Oh, Jack—

JACK

Leave me lone.

CURTAIN ACT II

ACT 3

scene one

a street, Chicago.

In the BLACKOUT, *at slow tempo, approaching from the distance, "How Long Blues": bass drum, clarinet, trombone. As the* LIGHTS COME UP, NEGROES *are quietly filling the stage;* THEY *arrange themselves as if lining both sides of a street. A few* POLICEMEN *station themselves among them, and a group of* PRESSMEN *is deployed at one side. The* FUNERAL PROCESSION *appears, the* BANDSMEN *first, followed by the coffin—*GOLDIE *conspicuous as a pallbearer—behind it* CLARA, *supported by* SISTER, *then the* PASTOR. *The* MUSIC *stops as the coffin is set down. The* NEGROES *close in around it and the* PASTOR *addresses them.*

PASTOR

"When thou passes through de waters Ah will be wid
  thee,
and de rivers, dey shall not overflow thee,
fo Ah am de Lawd thy God, de Holyone of Isrel."

CONGREGATION

Amen.

PASTOR

Mosta you ain present today outa respec to Sistah Tiny
  here,
you-all here to stan up fo son Jack. An dass fine!
He got a place in you heart, de Lawd muss wan him
  havin it.

173

But Bredren, make a place dere fo dis humble woman,
    his momma, too.
Take Sistah in you heart an let her show you somethin,
    Bredren,
Ah know you done took in what Jack bin showin you,
but dis leass as good an mebbe worth more,
praise de Lawd.

CONGREGATION
Amen.

PASTOR
"When thou passes through de waters Ah will be wid
    thee."
Dis woman pass through dem all de days of her life.
Born slave, like lotsa you poppas and mommas.
Passed through dem waters. Passed through plain hun-
    gry waters,
mean waters, cesspool-y waters. Currents like to swamp
    you—

CONGREGATION
Lawd!

PASTOR
Waters wid blood in em! Even passed through de waters
of dat killer flood down Galveston, passin through one
    waters
inter de nex one—

CONGREGATION
Lawd!

PASTOR
Sweatin in dem waters
fum "cain't see" in de mornin till "cain't see" at night,
an inter de nex one—

CONGREGATION
Jesus!

PASTOR

An when she coulden sweat no mo,
passed through em juss shiverin an achin an sick—
but whut wuz going long wid her!

CONGREGATION

Mah Savior!

PASTOR

Tell me dat!

CONGREGATION

Glory comin!

PASTOR

Amen!
De Lawd say Ah'll be wid thee,
de Lawd was passin through dem waters wid her,
inter de nex one an de nex one an de nex,
holdin her afloatin an liftin up de joy in her—

CONGREGATION

Hallelujah!

PASTOR

DASS whut she had, Bredren! Dass whut she show you!
She din cuss dem waters—

CONGREGATION

No, Lawd!

PASTOR

She know whut evvybody know in deir heart here,
dere's ALWAYS dem waters, dere ALWAYS tribberla-
tion,
de nex one an de nex
an we ALWAYS passin through—

CONGREGATION

Can't hurt me!

PASTOR

Ah is, an you is,
an you chillun gonna, an anybody's chillun
till kingdom come—

CONGREGATION

Oh, yeah!

PASTOR

She din blame de Lawd
fo not partin dem waters like de ole Red Sea!
She knowed He done said, "Dey shall not overflow thee,"
an she TRUSTED her Lawd.

CONGREGATION

Jesus!

PASTOR

She knowed dat fifty year ago
when we wuz nigh to GITTIN overflowed
He give us a Moses an He did part dat sea
an He took us outa bondage!

CONGREGATION

Hallelujah!

PASTOR

She knowed
All de time she pine for her boy
dat de Lawd workin in His own way—

(CLARA *begins sobbing*)

dat He ain't juss on tap evvy time we give a holler—

CONGREGATION

Oh my!

PASTOR

She felt de Lawd takin her fore she got ta see him,
but she held on tight to dat—

(Flurry of movement, photo-flashes, jostling)

NEGRO 1

Whut gawn on dere—

PHOTOGRAPHER 1

This way, miss—

PHOTOGRAPHER 2

Excuse me—

GOLDIE

Say, can't you guys—

CLARA *(going for*
PHOTOGRAPHER 1)

Gimme dat, you mother—

PASTOR

Sistah—

NEGRO 2

Who dat—

GOLDIE *(checking HER)*

For Godsakes—

POLICEMAN 1

No shoving there—

PASTOR

Gennulmen—

CLARA

Leggo me—

GOLDIE

Ignore em, just—

CLARA

You too, ya dirty pinkface pimp—

PASTOR

Sistah, dis ain no time—

CLARA (*breaking away*)
Yeah, oh yeah
dis de time awright! Whut he doin here,
whut any of em doin here—

SISTER
Clara—

CLARA
Look at em!
Howya feelin now, folks! All dress up dere
watchin de fewnral? Ain'tya bought some flowahs?

GOLDIE (*to* PASTOR)

I'm sorry about this—

CLARA
Sho you is!
You an dat white bitch an de whole pack a ya—
come on ovah to de box here, sugah,
see how good y'all nail de lid down—

PASTOR

Sistah—

CLARA
No!
Ah seed mah Momma Tiny's heart gittin busted,
Ah seed her layin dere pinin and sick
till she nothin but bone, Ah heard her beggin fo Jack—
Who set him runnin! Who put de mark on him!
Why she die so bad! Where all her trouble fum!
Dem, dem, dem, dem, an Ah wanna make
juss one of em—

(*Goes for the audience*)

PASTOR
Sistah—

(*Struggle*)

POLICEMAN 1 (*to* PASTOR)
Look, if you can't handle em—

PASTOR
Bredren—

NEGRO 2
No, let her, man—

CLARA
Ah gonna settle wid—

SISTER (*slaps* CLARA's *face*)
Behave yourself!

CLARA (*falling on the coffin*)
Oh help me, Momma Tiny, Ah wanna do right by ya,
Don' leave me, Momma, Momma, Ah be good, please . . .

PASTOR
Oh, brudders and sistahs!
Look out when Satan start a-lightin dat hate fire!
Member who de Lawd say vingeance belong ta,
member he fogit not de cry a de oppressed—

SCIPIO (*concealed in the* CROWD)
Dass right, chillun, suffer nice an easy—
school em on it, boss!

PASTOR
Who talkin dere!

SCIPIO (*appearing*)
Me—
ya no-name brudder!

PASTOR
Take dat off your head here—

SCIPIO
No! Went inta buy me a hat once, boss,
Man say cover you head wid a hankie
And DEN try it on—

PASTOR
Shame on you!

SCIPIO
Yeah, now you sayin it—shame on me, an shame on alla
    us
for BEIN de oppressed, an bein it, an bein it!
Shame on us moanin low two hunnerd years here!
Fo needin a big White Moses fo a daddy!

NEGRO 3
                              Amen, brudder!

PASTOR
Whut—

SCIPIO
    Yeah!
Shame on evvy Goodie-Book thumper like you!
White man keep pullin de teeth outa you head
an preacher here giving you de laughin-gas—

PASTOR
Ah warnin you, heathen—

SCIPIO
            Ah warnin evvybody!
Warnin dat white gal an warnin dem po-lice
ain nothin lass foever!

NEGRO 2
Tell em!

SCIPIO
                    Warnin dat dead woman
Jesus wuzn't swimmin! Warnin mah people
dat boy juss a shadow an dey livin black men
whut gotta live long—

NEGRO 3
Right!

SCIPIO
                    Don' Amen me!
Makin believe you de Chillun of Isrel,
fiery-furnacin an roll-on-Jordanin—
you ain no Isrel! Dere—

(*Points to* GOLDIE)

                    Dass a Jew-man—
see whut ya see! Look in de mirrah once
an see whut ya see! Ah said de MIRRAH,
not a lotta blue eyes you *usin* fo a mirrah,
an hatin whut dey hates, de hair you got,
de nose you got, de mouth you got, de—

PASTOR
Offissah, Ah'm askin you—

POLICEMAN 1
Right—

NEGRO 3
Whut dey doin—

SCIPIO
Hate dat woolly head, you gotta hate de man whut got
    it, brudders,
dat man YOU—

POLICEMAN 2 (*to* SCIPIO)
        Move—

SCIPIO

Don' hate it, brudders—

NEGRO 5

Lemme through—

NEGRO 6

Stop em—

SCIPIO (*as* POLICE *haul at him*)

Champeen in your heart, but dey ain one a you—

NEGRO 4

Help him—

NEGRO 6

Dey hurtin him—

NEGRO 7

Quick—

NEGRO 8

Dey gonna kill him—

NEGRO 4

Let em have it—

POLICEMAN 3

Move—

PASTOR

Bredren—

NEGRO 1 (*holding back*
CLARA)

Sistah—

NEGRO 5

No cuttin—

NEGRO WOMAN 1

Help—

NEGRO 8

Cut em—

POLICEMAN 3

There—

NEGRO 4

Gimme dat—

POLICEMAN 1

Come on, call em out—!

(POLICE WHISTLES *above the pandemonium; flashing nightsticks and swinging fists; the coffin is hurried off;* LIGHTS BEGIN FADING *and* HOOFBEATS *are heard, then* SCREAMS)

NEGRO VOICES

Look out—
No, dis way—
Brudders—
Pull em off—
No—
You mother—
Here—
Lemme git one—
Move—
Teddy—
Run—
Here—
Mah head, mah head, mah head, mah head—

(DARKNESS. *Silence.* LIGHTS UP *on*—)

scene two

Pop Weaver's office, New York.

CAP'N DAN *and* SMITTY, *followed in by* POP *and* FRED. *Newspapers.*

CAP'N DAN

Look at this, look at this—**I can't even think straight—**

SMITTY

I told you, he's out for—

CAP'N DAN

Don't tell me again!
One more lousy picture of him and that belt,
One more newsie sneakin down there to see him—

FRED

What about the ones on me up here, Dan'l?

CAP'N DAN

Say you can't promote it! Say he's askin too much!

FRED

After that piece in the *Journal?*

SMITTY

Here.

FRED

Will Fight Kid for Carfare and a Watermelon.

CAP'N DAN

Christ—

POP

Maybe we could pay him off to retire, Dan—

CAP'N DAN

Twenty years, what I'd give for twenty years—

POP

He wouldn't need to lay down, we'd get the belt back—

CAP'N DAN

Sure, and have a coon champ retire undefeated!

SMITTY

What if we promise him a straight fight later on
if he dives on this one.

FRED

Later on.

SMITTY

You know.

CAP'N DAN

He's too goddam smart for that!

FRED

Just an idea now,
but supposing we sign it, then something gets put
on his sponge, or in his water . . .

SMITTY

It's worked before, Dan.

POP

I would hate to hang this on something from a drug-
store.

CAP'N DAN

Jesus, listen to us, look what that boogie's
got us down to here—

POP
Don't excite yourself, Dan—

CAP'N DAN
On the verge, I tell them! You know what I look like,
stalling for months and making excuses,
and all he winds up is smack on the border
like a boil on the whole country's ass?

FRED
                    All right!
Then why don't we sign it and have it, for chrissake!
He'll never be in shape the way he was in Reno—

CAP'N DAN
Get it in writing—

FRED
            Here, look at the gut on him—
And look at that Kid—

POP
Fred—

FRED
Honest to God, he's better, every time out, listen,
four KO's and three decisions since April,
and I've got him with Brady now,
we've giving him all kinds of angles on the nigger,
like how when he smiles—

CAP'N DAN
            Do I have to hear this?

FRED
Wait, no, I mean it—when you're doin a smile, see,
your mouth's kina open and your teeth's not clenched,
so you hit him when he's smilin, you can bust a guy's
    jaw—
That's no bull, that's from an osteopath!

CAP'N DAN

Pop, you try, go down there yourself—

POP

Dan, I don't discourage very easy,
But I'm afraid there's only one safe bet for us.
It isn't ideal—

CAP'N DAN
Come on, come on—

POP

Even if he's still as good as he was, Dan,
the man is no spring chicken any more.
And you know what happens. Maybe not by tomorrow,
or the next day either, but it will happen, Dan.
The legs'll start to go, like everybody else's—
it's all downhill.

CAP'N DAN
Two years? Three years?

POP

Whenever he's ripe we throw him in with Fred's boy—

CAP'N DAN

Pop, can't you help me?

POP

Taking this on was a real mistake, Dan.
I'd like to follow through but that's the best we have.

FRED

I'd go along—

SMITTY
We could say we're waiting
on account of the war—

FRED
We could give a big play
to the middleweights—

CAP'N DAN
Pop—Jesus!

POP
We can work it,
let's put it on ice—

CAP'N DAN
There ain't that much ice
in this whole rotten world—

FRED
What do we do then—
kill him?

(*Pause*)

CAP'N DAN
How broke is he, Smitty?

SMITTY
They live in a flophouse
and he trains in a barn.

CAP'N DAN
Any dough from outside?

SMITTY
Friends, a little.

CAP'N DAN
Find out who, we'll stop it—
anybody sparring with him?

POP
Dan, what's the point—

SMITTY

A couple of rubes from Texas—

CAP'N DAN
Pull them out, send them home.
No exhibitions, nothing, no contact, cut him off—

POP

He's not going to give, Dan—

CAP'N DAN
He made the last
move he had and now we'll screw him with it,
now we're gonna show him
what a bad move it was, this time we ain't askin,
or offerin, or tryin, or pussyfootin round this
like a bunch of pansies, we got him so close
we can reach out and squeeze—**we're gonna squeeze
 that dinge**
so goddam hard soon a fix is gonna look
like a hayride to him!

POP
Dan, don't get him
any madder than he is—

CAP'N DAN
Start scouting out
a place we can hold it—

POP
We're making us two
mistakes in a row, Dan—

CAP'N DAN
Havana, maybe,
the bigger the better—

POP
I mean it. Tell your people
we just can't deliver.

CAP'N DAN

No, I tell them
we might need a hand—

FRED

Say, wait—

CAP'N DAN

You get busy,
talk to Goldie—I want all that set!

POP

We're way out over our head now, you know.

CAP'N DAN

So is he, friend. Let's see who goes under.

(BLACKOUT. *Enter* CLARA *in* SPOTLIGHT, *as distant*
BELL *slowly chimes midnight.* SHE *clutches a flimsy*
stained garment to her)

CLARA

Do it, soon, soon, goin good now, drag him
on down. Oh won'tya, fo me an mah momma
an evvy black-ass woman he turn his back on,
for evvy gal wid a man longside dreamin him
a piece a what HE got, fo alla his let-down
secon-bess sistahs, all Mistah Number One's
lil ugly sistahs—ssh!—
dey' moonin fo de day you does it,
dey's some sleepin an plenny itchin quiet,
dey's me aholda dis, an we drawin him,
drawin him. Oh, where dem rosy
cheeks gonna git him, don' never stop now,
offa dat high horse an on down de whole
long mud-track in fronna him, years gawnta nothin,
feelin em, dere, limpin an slippin
an shrinkin an creepin an sinkin right in—
Call him to ya, Momma!

(Holds out the garment at full length: a nightgown, stiff with blood and excrement)

Soon, baby, soon.

(LIGHT fades slowly into BLACKOUT; thudding of a punching-bag is heard; LIGHTS UP on—)

scene three

a disused barn, Juarez.

By the light of a few kerosene lanterns, JACK pounds at a punching-bag, which is steadied from behind by PACO, a Mexican boy. TICK claps his hands in time with him.

TICK

Slow it up, slow it up—

JACK
Whut—?

TICK
                    Slow it,
let dat sweat out—

(Claps at a slower tempo, sings)

Times is very hard,
Gimme ten-cent worth a lard,
Gonna keep mah skillet greasy
If Ah can, can, can,
Gonna keep mah skillet—

(JACK *delivers a last impatient slam and turns away from it*)

Nuff?

TICK

Yeah, Ah'm pushin.

TICK
OK, Paco, dassit.

JACK
Six-thirty mañana.

PACO
Si, Campeón. We ron?

JACK
Yeah, we run.

PACO
I com for wek op?

JACK
No, Ah be up.

(PACO *starts putting gear in order*)

TICK (*leading* JACK *to
a trestle table*)
Wearin us out, baby, comin on fine . . .

(JACK *sits,* TICK *pulls his gloves off*)

Oughta raise de bag up higher tomorrer,
startya liftin em, huh?

(JACK *lies down*)

Yeah . . .

(*Working on him*)

bout a foot or so. You know, seein how big dat Kid is . . .

(JACK *does not reply*)

Sho a funny size for a Kid, ain he?
Soun like somethin gone wrong wid his glans!

> JACK
>
> Don' try unwindin me, man. Juss rub.

>> TICK
>>
>> Yassuh, shine em up—

>>> JACK (*to* PACO, *who has
>>>   picked up his gloves*)
>>>   Leave dose, willya.

>> PACO
>>
>> Si, Campeón.

>>> TICK
>>>   You cain work out
>>> tonight no mo, Ah mean—

>>> JACK
>>>   How much dat guy say
>>> he giveya for em.

>>> TICK
>>>   Oh.

>>> JACK
>>>   Fifty?

(BARKING *is heard*)

>>> TICK
>>>
>>> You gloves, baby.

(JACK *doesn't reply*)

PACO *(looking out)*
Viene la señorita.

JACK
Put em in a piece a paper she don' see em.

TICK
Well, you kin work wid de heavy ones, time bein.
Bettah fo ya, anyhow.

(*More* BARKING. ELLIE *enters, carrying a dish with a napkin over it.* SHE *wears sunglasses*)

PACO
Buenas noches—

TICK
Mmm-MM!
Whut dat old lanlady whip up tonight?

PACO *(at the door shooing
away the dogs)*
Andale! Vaya!

ELLIE
I wish they would feed their dogs around here.

JACK
You feedin yours here, ain'tya.

TICK *(resuming massage)*
Set it down, hon—
how mah gal today?

ELLIE
All right. You?

TICK
Fine!

Shoulda seed him burn up dat road dis mornin,
right fum de bridge to Pedrilla an up ta—

> JACK (*to* ELLIE, *not
> looking at her*)

Gonna say it or whut.

> ELLIE
> No, nothing, Jack.

No cables. Nothing.

> JACK
> Thanks.

> TICK
> Man, we be hearing pretty soon.

Worry juss makin you tight, dass why
ya ain sweatin like ya oughta—

> JACK
> Juss you rub, man.

> TICK

Ass me, we's lucky dey ain sign it up yet!
Givin us all dis good gittin-ready time?

> ELLIE

Let him eat before it gets cold, Tick.

> TICK

Yeah, switch you brain off a while an—

> JACK
> Leave it.

> TICK

OK, OK.

  (*Long pause*)

ELLIE

Jack—

(TRAIN WHISTLE)

PACO

Tren from El Paso.

ELLIE
Yes?

TICK

Yeah . . . Whistle like dat crossin ovah.

PACO

Hasta mañana, señores.

TICK
So long, kid.

(PACO *goes*)

ELLIE

Why don't you come back and wash now, Jack.
I'll wait here if you like.

JACK
Smelling pretty strong, huh?

ELLIE

You know that's not what I—

JACK (*sitting up*)
Dass inuff, man.

ELLIE

Jack, will you talk to me.

JACK
Tick gawn ovah

on a erran, you kin go walk roun dere
a lil widdim—

ELLIE
No, I want to talk to you—

JACK
Mebbe git a ice-cream soda, lookit some
Mericans or somethin—

ELLIE
Jack—

TICK
                    Not wid me, boss—
Ah ain strollin wid no white gal in no Texas!

(*To* ELLIE, *as he goes out with the package*)

Hole de fort, hon, won' be too long.

(*Pause.* TRAIN WHISTLE)

ELLIE
Let them go ahead, Jack.

JACK
                    Take dem specs off.
Ah cain hardly see ya.

ELLIE (*doing so*)
I didn't think you wanted to.

JACK
You readin mah mine now?

ELLIE
            Jack—

JACK

Ah toleya
keep outa dis, din Ah.

ELLIE

I can't. Please,
let them, you have to.

JACK

Finely battin
fo de home team, huh.

ELLIE

Cable them tonight,
please—

JACK

Finely come roun to it—

ELLIE

Jack, don't bitch me now—

JACK

Ah toleya—

ELLIE

No, I don't care!
Forget what you told me! Say yes and get it
over with, for God's sake! You're letting them
do this to you, it's worse—

JACK

Worse fo you, mebbe—

ELLIE

Jack, it's slow poison here, there's nothing else to wait
    for,
just more of it, you've had enough—please,
you're being paralyzed—

JACK
Wid you mebbe—

ELLIE
All right, yes, with me too,
with everything but hammering that stupid bag there!
You're not your own man any more—

JACK
Now you rollin—

ELLIE
How can you be your own man, they have you!
They do and you know it, you're theirs, at least
you can buy yourself back from them—

JACK
Sold—
one-buck nigger fo de lady!

ELLIE
Let it sound the way it is!
Run when they push you and back when they pull you,
work yourself sick in this hell-hole for nothing,
and tell me you're not theirs—here,
look at the grease you swallow for them,
look at the bedbug bites on your arms,
and the change in your pockets and the blotches in
your eyes—

JACK
Don' leave de smell out—

ELLIE
The two of us smell!
Whatever turns people into niggers—there—

(*Shows her neck*)

it's happening to both of us—

JACK
    Wish comin true, huh—

ELLIE
                         No,
never this, it wasn't this—

JACK
    Sing it, sistah!

ELLIE
I want you there fighting them again,
that's what I wish now, I want to watch
when you're knocking them down for this, dozens of
    them,
God help them, wipe it off on all of them—

JACK
How bout rooster-fightin, plenty right here—

ELLIE
Listen to me, please—

JACK
    Oughta look inta dat—

ELLIE
You'd fight them and you'd be with your friends and
    you'd—

(JACK *crows like a rooster*)

JACK
            Somebody wanna sign me?

ELLIE
Maybe we could live then, damn you!

JACK
            Lil frame house,
tree in front?

ELLIE

Anything!

JACK

Nice quiet street?

ELLIE

Anywhere! A place!

JACK

Lil cozy—

ELLIE

A kitchen!

JACK

Put de cat out? Tuck in de kids?

ELLIE

Oh, you're just hateful!

JACK

Well Ah gonna tellya whut de livin like, baby,
far as Ah concern—

ELLIE

Get away from me—

JACK

Yeah,
Ah put you straight on it—an alla you, too.
Ah wen into a fair once and dere wuz dis old pug, see,
give anybody two bucks who stan up a roun widdim—
perfessional set-up, reggerlation ring an all,
cep dey had rope juss on three sides, dass right,
de back side wuz de tent. So Ah watches a couple
git laid out real quick in dere, but he don' look
dat red-hot ta me, see, so Ah climbs in widdim.
An Ah doin awright fo a youngster, when all it once
he bulls me up gainss dat tent-side a de ring

an SLAM, WHAM, somebody behine dere conks me,
right through de canvas, musta use a two by four,
an evvy time Ah stans up he shove me back agin,
an SLAM, dere's anudder, down she come—
good story, huh?

ELLIE

Jack—

JACK

Dass how it go like Ah knows it, baby—

ELLIE

Sometimes, sometimes—

JACK

All de way now!
dass where Ah is and dass whut Ah'm gittin,
gonna git it de same sayin Yassuh, Nossuh,
don' mattah whut Ah does—Ah in dere, unnerstan?
An Ah don' wan you watchin, or helpin, or waitin,
or askin, or hannin me you jive bout livin,
or anythin fromya but OUT, Ah mean OUT—

ELLIE

What—

JACK

How goddamn plain Ah gotta make it for ya!

ELLIE

Jack—if you want other girls—

JACK

Git you stuff ready,
train out ten o'clock.

ELLIE

No, no, I won't, no—

JACK

When Tick come Ah sen him ovah—

ELLIE

                              Jack—

JACK

                              Bettah start movin—

ELLIE

Stop it—

JACK

          Ah pologize actin so yellah
up ta—

ELLIE

          Wait, you have to stop it—

JACK

All Ah has to is be black an die, lady—

ELLIE

I want to stay, even if we—

JACK

Stay wid you own, lady—

ELLIE

                    What are you doing!

JACK

Quit dat, quit it, short an sweet—

ELLIE

                              I won't go—

JACK

You knowed it comin, start movin—

ELLIE

Wait—

JACK

Don' cross me now—

ELLIE

Jack, I thought we'd
save something, please—

JACK

Ah said MOVE—

ELLIE

Please, I only—

JACK

MOVE! You through widdit now—

ELLIE

Jack—

JACK

No mo lousy grub you gotta puke up,
no more a ya lookin like a wash-out rag here,
wid you eye twitchin alla—

ELLIE

Don't—I don't care—

JACK

Juss MOVE—

ELLIE

I'll take better—

JACK

Hangin on me,
dead weight—

ELLIE
No, not for you—

JACK
Start—

ELLIE
Jack, I'll find a job, please—

JACK
Ah toleya when mah momma die, Ah toleya
leave me be a while, now—

ELLIE
Jack, I can't
run anymore, not by myself—

JACK
You got you people
and you a—

ELLIE
No, listen—

JACK
You a young woman
an you gonna—

ELLIE
Please, I'd never—

JACK
Gonna fine—

ELLIE
No one else, I'd—

JACK
Tough titty—

ELLIE

Just—

JACK

Move,
or goddamn you—

ELLIE

Why can't you wait at least!
Wait till you've given me a chance to make you happy—
one chance, only one—**I swear I've never had one**—

JACK

Too big a order all aroun!

ELLIE

No, I won't go—

JACK

Wanna drag it out, huh—

ELLIE

I won't, I can't—

JACK

Den Ah gonna wise you up good now, you gray bitch—

ELLIE

You can't make me go, stop doing this—

JACK

Why you think
Ah ain't put a han to yo fo how long, why ya think
it turn me off juss lookin atya—

ELLIE

Stop it—

JACK

You stayin,
stay fo it all. Ya know why?

Does ya, honeybunch? Cause evvy time you pushes
dat pinch-up face in fronna me, Ah sees
where it done got me, dass whut Ah lookin at,
where an how come an de Numbah One Who,
right down de line, girl, an Ah mean YOU,
an Ah don' wanna give you NOTHIN, unnerstan?
Ah cut it off firss!

ELLIE

Oh, I despise you—

JACK

Right, like alla resta ya—

ELLIE

Oh, I'd like to smash you—

JACK

Me an evvy udder dumb nigger who'd letya!
Now go on home an hustle one up who don' know it yet,
plenny for ya, score em up—watch out, brudders!
Oughta hang a bell on so dey hear you comin.

ELLIE

You mean this?

JACK

Look in mah purple eyes.

(Pause)

ELLIE

You win, daddy.

(SHE turns and goes. Pause. JACK takes a swig from
the water-bottle, gargles, spits, then walks to the
punching-bag and starts to jab at it. For a few moments HE does not notice the entrance of a slightly
shabby but imposing-looking Mexican, EL JEFE.
Then, sensing someone behind him, JACK stops)

EL JEFE
I leesen you mek beeg denuncio, Campeón.
So I nut com een.

JACK
Who you, mistah?

EL JEFE
Ees nut meester, Campeón. I seet now, yes?

(Sits)

JACK
Whut you want?

EL JEFE (taking out a bottle
and offering it)
You like?

JACK
No, Ah'm in trainin.

EL JEFE
Pliz?

JACK
Trainin. On a fight.

EL JEFE
Si, es terrible . . .
for Negro, for peon, for avery poor peoples.
fight from meenit we out from dee modder.

JACK
Ah astya whut you want, man.

EL JEFE
I hear, Campeón. Salud.

(Drinks)

JACK
Look, Ah ain made no trouble wid none a you.

EL JEFE *(laughs a bit)*
Where ees dee fadders, compadre.

JACK
De whut?

EL JEFE
Dee fadders. Dee weengs. Ees all high ovair
flying like anjel, you think, no? **El hombre solo.**

JACK
Whut you after, man?

EL JEFE
Maybe you halp soon
pobre black amigos. You show heem
ees solo nut posible . . . Que vida, eh?

JACK *(moving to the door)*
Man, you juss playin wid me, Ah'm gonna—

EL JEFE *(standing)*
No,
I filling to you beeg compassion, my fran.
Dees Mejico my cowntry, I ongry here, I keel here,
I am fugitivo like you much times. Bot ulways to love.
You cowntry you nut love her and she nut you,
unly mak bad drims ich odder.

(A CAR *has been approaching and is heard braking*)

VOICE OUTSIDE
Han venido, Jefe.

EL JEFE
Déjanlos entrar.

(*Pause. Enter* DIXON, GOLDIE, *and a young* AGENT)

DIXON

Good evening.

EL JEFE

Señores.

GOLDIE

Hello, Jack.

JACK

Yeah.

OK. Ah'm listenin.

GOLDIE

Well . . .

(*To* DIXON)

All right?

(DIXON *impassive*)

They're makin it easier, Jack. I mean it's . . .
They threw in now suspended sentence.

JACK

Yeah.

GOLDIE

You fight in Havana, you hand yourself in,
you go to court, one-two-three, and that's all.

JACK

Go on, boss.

GOLDIE

Well . . .

JACK

Don' be shy bout it.

GOLDIE

Jackie, it's quits now . . .

(*Stops, pained*)

JACK (*to* DIXON)
Mebbe you tell me.

DIXON

Apart from your original conviction, Jefferson,
which carries, you remember, up to three years,
there are quite a few other violations, involving,
for example: jumping bail, using the mails
to bribe officials in Canada, tax irregularities,
falsifying passports—

GOLDIE
They'll throw the whole book on you.
Till God knows when.

JACK
Tell me de ress of it, mistah.
You law up dere an Ah down here. Cain leave dat out—

(*To* EL JEFE)

Can he, man? You country, ain't it, man?

EL JEFE (*downcast*)
Si, compadre.

AGENT
It is perfectly legal,
once we've ascertained where a wanted man is,
to request cooperation of the parties in charge there.

EL JEFE
Perdóname, Campeón. We nid from dem, comprende?
We nut like. We nid.

JACK
Yeah.

EL JEFE
Go Habana. Ees batter.

DIXON
I would think so.

GOLDIE
You finish inside there,
what'll you have, Jack. **An old man he'll be.**

JACK
Well . . . Ah'm far long awready, boss.
Ah'm stannin here gittin older evvy minnit.
An Ah'm goin right through dat door—

(*Moves*)

EL JEFE
No—

(*Draws pistol*)

compadre!

(*Steps in front of* JACK)

JACK
Use it if ya got to, man.

EL JEFE
Hombre, ivin I lat you, where now you—

JACK
Dassall up to me, man.

(*Advances*)

EL JEFE
I tie weeth rope, you do theess—!

JACK
Oh, Ah killya firss, man.

(*Advances*)

EL JEFE
Hijo, averyplace
catch on you, I swear you, all geev you to gringos,
Huerta, Obregón—

JACK (*advancing*)
Ah goin out de door, man—

EL JEFE
Hombre . . .

(*Clicks back hammer*)

Hombre—

JACK
Gimme a break, fo Gawdsake.

EL JEFE
                                                    No!
Who you halpeeng een your life, nadie,
OSS now you halp—

(JACK *advances*)

Cabrón, wan more—

JACK
                                        Well,
mebbe it be doin me a favor.

(*Steps around* EL JEFE, *keeps walking*)

GOLDIE
Jack—

(EL JEFE *raises his pistol*)

DIXON
In the leg—

AGENT
Don't—

EL JEFE
Chíngate, gringo—

(*Aims at* JACK's *back, calls*)

You stuppeeng? Hombre, nut stuppeeng, I—

(JACK *at the doorway, suddenly stops, then slowly moves backward as* TICK *and* TWO MEXICANS *enter.* THEY *carry in* ELLIE's *mud-smeared and dripping body*)

MEXICAN
Se tiró en el pozo. Acabada.

EL JEFE
Díos.

JACK
Whut . . . whut . . . ?

TICK
Threw hersel down de . . .

JACK
No, no, Jesus—

TICK
Down de well, Ah coulden—

JACK

                                        Git somebody,
gimme de bottle—why she—

TICK
                    Busted her neck, man.

JACK

                                        Honey!
Honey, baby, please, sugar, no—!
Whut Ah—whut Ah—whut Ah—baby,
whut Ah done to ya, whut you done, honey,
honey, whut dey done to us . . .

EL JEFE (*turns away*)
                    No puedo mirarlo.

GOLDIE
Jack. Jack. Anything I can . . .

        (JACK *nods*)

                        Anything. What, Jack.

JACK
Set dat fuckin fight up! Set it up, set it up!
Ah take it now!

        (BLACKOUT. *Sound of* PRESSES *rolling.* CAP'N DAN *appears in* SPOTLIGHT: HE *smokes a cigar, wears a white
        carnation, carries a small valise, and is jubilant*)

CAP'N DAN
Well, there's such a commotion on this
you'd think we just organized the Second Coming!
Tickets? They're going down without em, hey,
honest to God, it does your heart good,
songs about the Kid, pictures of the Kid
stuck up in windows, stores, you pass a brick wall
it has KID painted on it, people on the street saying

Well we got the Hope, Dan!—cost me two hundred
in cigars already—and wait, wait,
I bet you can't guess who's refereein—Brady!
Oh, will they eat that up, when he's givin the count
and he's—what? No, he ain't in on it,
neither is the Kid, who the hell wants that!
But he's the one who lost it,
and the whole world's gonna see him
take it in his hand again, and hold it up
and pass it on, like the Kid'll pass it—

    (BOAT WHISTLE *interrupts him*)

                                  OK!
This time we'll keep it in the family!

    (DAN *exits*)

scene four

a street, somewhere in the United States.

As DAN *exits a group of* NEGROES *swarms on,* ONE *of
them rapidly beating on a bass drum,* ANOTHER *holding up a torch in one hand and a pail in the other,
a* THIRD *scribbling on a long sheet of foolscap; the*
OTHERS *clamorously surround them, calling out their
names and throwing money into the pail.* DRUMMING
throughout.

                  NEGRO 1
Oscar Jones—

                  NEGRO 2
Pearl Whitney—

NEGRO 3
Jasper Smollett—

PAIL MAN
Write em down dere—throw in dem nickels—

NEGRO 4
Charlie Webb—

NEGRO 5
Bill Montgomery—

PAIL MAN
More! Who else here—
Sign on de telgram to Jack—fi' cents—

NEGRO 4
Read out de message, man—

NEGRO 1
Let em all hear it!

PAIL MAN
"HELLO JACK BESS NACHUL FIGHTER IN DE WORL—"

(*Cheers*)

"HOME FOLKS PUNCHIN RIGHT WIDYA— SIGNED—"

(*The* CHEERING *drowns him, a* VOICE *over it sings—*)

VOICE
Hot boilin sun comin ovuh—

NEGRO 6
Waltuh Peters!

SEVERAL JOINING IN
Hot boilin sun comin ovuh—

NEGRO 2
We show ya!

MORE JOINING
Hot boilin sun comin ovuh—

NEGRO 7
Ah'm on dere!

ALL (*singing*)
AN HE AIN'T A-COMIN DOWN—

(*Whooping and cheering,* THEY *run off, the sound of their* VOICES *fading into the* ROAR *of the* CROWD *as* LIGHTS COME UP *on*—)

scene five

Oriente Racetrack, Havana.

Entrance gate. Two huge ornate wooden columns; suspended high between them, a banner featuring the simplified figures of a white boxer and a black one locked in combat. A cluster of ticketless WHITE MEN *at the barrier,* ALL *feverishly trying to follow the fight by the roars of the crowd and through* ONE *of their number perched high on a column. In the fierce heat all coats have been discarded, most shirts as well; heads are bound with handkerchiefs or covered with cheap straw hats—a few of these still left are hawked by a couple of ragged* CUBAN NEGRO BOYS.

MAN 1 *(on column)*
No, Kid—block him—you're lettin him—

(ROAR)

MAN 2
Again?

MAN 3
Sounds like he—

MAN 1
No—but the dinge
caught him right in the—Kid! Christ—

MAN 4
What—?

MAN 1
Don't back up—

MAN 6 *(through paper
megaphone)*
Use them arms already—

MAN 7
Ten goddam rounds,
ain't took a one yet—

(ROAR, *as a* PINKERTON MAN *helps* MAN 8, *a sunstroke
victim, through the gate)*

PINKERTON MAN 1
I toldya—
leave the gate clear—

(ROAR)

MAN 1
Another one—

MAN 4

Just keep him
off you—

(POP *appears at a side door.* MAN 8 *doubles over, retching*)

PINKERTON MAN 1
Move—it's like an oven here—

MAN 6

Time, for chrissake—

NEGRO BOY 1 (*shaking a gourd in* MAN 8's *face*)
Eh! Eh! Eh! Eh!

MAN 1

Kid, quit clinchin—

MAN 8
Scram, ya dirty little—

MAN 1

BELL!

MAN 9

Thank God!

MAN 2
How the hell can he take it!

SMITTY (*coming through a side door*)
Jesus, Pop—

POP
You sure they got the high sign?

SMITTY
Two rounds ago!

POP

Then what—

SMITTY

Pop, I gave it four times, I know they
got it, Goldie flicked the towel, Pop, we went
over and over it—

MAN 4 (*to* MAN 1)

How's it look—

MAN 1

He's collapsin there
but so is the nigger—puffin like a goddamn buffalo—

MAN 2

He won't last—

MAN 6

Start sweatin blood, coon!

(FRED, *sweating and frantic, comes through side
door*)

FRED

I warned you, I warned you—

POP

Get back inside—

FRED

Can'tya—

SMITTY

Ssh!

POP

They won't cross us—

FRED

They nothing, it's HIM—

MAN 1

E-leven!

("Ooh" from CROWD *as* FRED *rushes back in)*

MAN 1

Right off, a low one—

MAN 7
You would, ya—

MAN 5

He can't help it,
the Kid's belly's five feet off the—

(ROAR)

MAN 1

Missed him, nigger—

(Enter the AGENT—*heads for* POP *and* SMITTY)

(ROAR)

MAN 1

He slipped, the nigger slipped—

(ROAR)

Hit him, hit him again—Oh, you—

MAN 3

What—

(POP *and* AGENT *whisper*)

MAN 1

Don't just look at him!

MAN 7
No instink! No instink!

(AGENT *whispers to* SMITTY; SMITTY *runs inside*)

MAN 4
Let's get mad, Kid—

MAN 7
A hundred and two degrees—
Chalkasians ain't made for it—

MAN 1
Oh, them clinches—

MAN 3
He holdin—?

MAN 1
Come—on—

(ROAR)

No, it's the nigger—! He's leanin, yeah—

MAN 4
He's wearin down!

MAN 3
I toleya—

MAN 1
Break it, ref—

MAN 2
Don't let him rest—

MAN 1
Oh, good man—

MAN 3
He wobblin—?

MAN 1
Sorta—yeah! Yeah!
He's backin away there, he's wipin his eyes—

MAN 6
Go in on him—

MAN 1
He's goin—the nigger ain't—there,
he's tryna dodge him—

(ROAR)

MAN 9
Run, tar-baby,
run back to your barrel—

MAN 1
Boyoboy, yeah,
he's slowin down, he's—

MAN 2
Let's go—

MAN 1
Shit—
move in—

(SMITTY *re-enters with* RUDY, *the baseball player*)

AGENT
OK, Rudy—

RUDY
Who you, man—

MAN 6
MOVE IN!

AGENT

Get your shirt off—

(*To* SMITTY)

get him something to carry—

(SMITTY *dashes back inside*)

RUDY

Mah whut?

AGENT (*tugging at the buttons*)
That! Off! Like you put one
on for him, remember—

MAN 1
No, Kid, chase him,
he's tryna get his wind back—

RUDY
Whut de hell you—

AGENT
Get into that corner, Rudy, tell that pal of yours—

(ROAR—*drowns what he says*)

MAN 1
Be care—no, jab him off ya—Christ,
the nigger's all over him, pile-drivin,
whalin at him—cover up, he's—duck—
Oh, Jesus, the Kid just—

RUDY (*as* SMITTY *returns
with towel and bottle*)
Gimme dat, you mother—

(*Seizes towel and bottle, and runs inside, pulling off
his shirt*)

MAN 1

Cover, Kid, turn, turn—cover, he'll cave
your ribs in—

(ROAR)

MAN 2

Stop the goddamn—

MAN 1

Wait, no, he's up—Oh
the nigger's right on him, he's after it, he's—

MAN 6

Kid, don't let him—

MAN 1

All he's got,
he's workin like a butcher—

MAN 2

No—

MAN 7

He's gotta—

MAN 5

Kid—Kid!—

MAN 9

Kid—

MAN 1

Hook in him,
sluggin—oh, that eye—

MAN 6

Ride him out—

(NEGRO BOY *climbs up the other column to see*)

MAN 7

Kid—

MAN 6

Bust your hand, you—

MAN 1

Murder, it's murder—

MAN 4

No more—

MAN 2

Clinch him—

MAN 1

Ref—

MAN 6

Clinch him, dummox—

MAN 2

No more—

MAN 1

REF!

MAN 5

Stop it—

MAN 2

REF, YA—

NEGRO BOY

Eh! Eh! Eh! Eh!

MAN 1

He's

on the ropes, he can't see, he's rollin,
he's punchy—

MAN 2
How the hell does he—

(ROAR)

MAN 6
Is he—

MAN 1
No, it's a bell, lemme down . . . lemme down . . .

(*Slips down the column:* MAN 4 *is helped up to take his place*)

POP (*to* SMITTY)
Tell Fred to throw in the—

AGENT (*to* SMITTY)
Stay right here!

MAN 4 (*looking ring-ward*)
God Almighty!

MAN 1 (*to* MAN 4)
They workin on the eye?

MAN 4
Yeah, but the rest of him—!
Blood, welts all over—

MAN 5
Fifty on the coon the next—

MAN 2
Shut your hole—

MAN 6
Don't worry, Kid—

MAN 1
That eye came up like a grape!

POP (*to* AGENT)
Oh, Mister—

PINKERTON MAN 1 (*offstage*)
Comin through—

(*Movement behind barrier*)

MAN 2
Jesus, the heat got him—

(PINKERTON MEN 1 *and* 2 *come through the gate carrying* GOLDIE *on a chair; the* AGENT *beckons to them*)

MAN 6
How you gonna fight without your Jew, spook—

GOLDIE (*to* AGENT)
Mister, it's no use, it's—

AGENT
Ssh!

MAN 4
Here they go—

(PINKERTON MEN *set* GOLDIE *down at the side door and run back inside*)

AGENT (*to* GOLDIE)
The boy get to him?

(ROAR)

MAN 4
Nigger's slouchin in there—

GOLDIE

Mister, he don't hear, he—

MAN 4

Little stiff on his pins there—
the Kid's just waiting for it—

GOLDIE

Like it's my son, I begged him!

MAN 4

The nigger's feelin him out—the Kid's sorta rockin
there—
back up, Kid—please—

(ROAR)

The nigger roundhoused him—!

MAN 5

Here it comes—

(ROAR)

The Kid's still up—
he's still up—tryna shake his head clear—
the nigger don't know where to—

(ROAR *changes*)

MAN 2

Stay on your feet—

MAN 7

Kid—

MAN 4

He is! He is! The nigger can't do it—
he's hittin but he's outa juice! He's punched out!

MAN 2

I knew it—

MAN 4
There! Nothin! Just stingin him,
slappin him—

MAN 1
Kid—

MAN 6
He can't hurtya—

MAN 1

He's arm-heavy—

MAN 9
Please, Kid—

MAN 4
Look at him—
He's saggin there, just heavin at you—

MAN 6

What the hell's he—

(ROAR)

MAN 4
He's hitting back!
He's lashin at him—swingin there wild—

MAN 1
He can't
see—

MAN 2
Kid—

MAN 4
The coon's givin ground—

MAN 7
                              Keep on
swingin—

MAN 4
There, the coon's lurchin
round him, he's—

MAN 6
Smell him out, Kid—

MAN 4
                              There—Oh—
swiped him half across the ring—

MAN 1 (*pulling down*
       NEGRO BOY)
                              Lemme up, you goddamn—

MAN 2
More—

MAN 3
It's gonna happen, Kid—

MAN 4
In on him, no, he's over—yeah—

MAN 7
                              Keep swinging—

MAN 4
Walkin in his sleep but he's after him—

MAN 6
                              Press him—

MAN 4

Just flailin them great big—

(ROAR)

Bango!

MAN 2

More, Kid!

MAN 7

Wheee!

MAN 1 *(on column)*

Christ, it's like a noctopus!

MAN 2

Don't stop, Kid—

MAN 4

Ya shot it all, coon, can't hurt him!

MAN 9

Wahooo!

MAN 6

Can't hurt nobody!

(GOLDIE *totters to his feet and goes back inside*)

MAN 1

Kid, aim it lower—

MAN 4

Don't have to, he's reelin—

MAN 2

Lower—

MAN 7

He'll go under you—

MAN 4
No—

got no legs left—

MAN 1
Bango!

MAN 2
Yippeee!

MAN 6

Give us the smile, coon—

MAN 1
He's flounderin—

MAN 2
Poleax him—

MAN 4

There—

MAN 1
Clap for that one, you—

MAN 4
Now, Kid—

MAN 2

Finish him—

MAN 1
The nigger can't hardly

get his guard up—

MAN 2
Finish him—

MAN 4
It's comin—
the Kid got him bulled into a corner—
punchin blind—

MAN 1
The blood's in both eyes—

MAN 2 (*and* OTHERS)
Now—now—now—

MAN 4
Just goin like a windmill—

MAN 7
Oh, flatten him—

MAN 2
Wipe the rotten—

MAN 4
There—
the nigger's grabbin for the rope—he's bucklin—
he's swingin with his other—

MAN 6
You're THROUGH—

MAN 4
The Kid's
poundin right down on him, he's grabbin,
he's hangin, he's holdin, he can't, the Kid's
drivin him down like a big black—

(*Great* ROAR: MAN 1 *follows the referee's count with
his own arm; his voice barely audible*)

MAN 1
Four—five—six—seven—eight—

(*The* CROWD'S ROAR *pulsates with the last two counts
and pandemonium breaks loose: hugging, dancing,
etc.*)

MAN 1   (*falling into arms
below*)

I love him, I love him—

(AGENT *leaves*)

MAN 2
Wahooo—

(POP *goes inside with* SMITTY)

MAN 6

We got it—

MAN 2
Yoweee—

MAN 6
Where's my fifty—

MAN 5
Let's get in there—

(THEY *all push at the barrier*)

MAN 2
What a Kid—

MAN 1
Quit the pushing—

(*Snatches of band music from within*)

MAN 4
They're bringin the nigger out—

MAN 2
Who cares—

MAN 6
Open up—

MAN 7
We're missin all the—

MAN 6
Break it in, for—

MAN 2 (*as* THEY *break through*)
W-A-A-H-O-O-OH!

(THEY ALL *rush in except* MAN 9, *who stops to throw a coin to* NEGRO BOY 2)

MAN 9
Here, chico—buy yourself a whitewash!

(HE *follows the rest and the* BOY *runs off. The sounds of jubilation within rise still higher: the remaining* NEGRO BOY *climbs the column to watch*)

PINKERTON MAN 2 (*offstage*)
Outa the way, come on, let 'em through here—

(JACK, *helped along by* TICK *and* GOLDIE *and escorted by four* PINKERTON MEN, *comes limping through the gates, the* PRESS *at his heels*)

PRESSMAN 1
Just a word, Jack—

PINKERTON MAN 2
Let's go boys—

GOLDIE
Not now—

PRESSMAN 2
Jack, in the tenth when you were—

(*The music and crowd noise suddenly dwindle, and the faint but triumphant sound of the* ANNOUNCER'S VOICE *is heard.* JACK *stops*)

TICK
Les go, baby.

(JACK *stands listening*)

PRESSMAN 3
Jack—why do you think it happened?

(JACK *stands listening*)

I'm asking—

(*The* VOICE *rises to its conclusion: great cheering: the* BOY *climbs down.* JACK *turns to* PRESSMAN 3)

Why did it, Jack?

JACK
He beat me, dassall.
Ah juss din have it.

(*The* BOY *spits on him and darts away*)

Ain't dat right, boy?

TICK (*moving him on*)
Take it slow, nice an slow . . .

PRESSMAN 3
But why, Jack? Really.

JACK (*laughs, stops*)
Oh, man.

Ah ain't got dem reallies from de Year One . . .
An if any a you got em, step right down an say em.

(*Looks around at audience:* DRUM-BEATING *begins*)

No . . . you new here like Ah is—

(MUSIC: *A March Triumphal*)

Come on Chillun!
Let 'em pass by!

> (*Spreading his arms,* HE *sweeps* TICK, GOLDIE, *and
> 1 or 2* PRESSMEN *off to one side, moving slowly, as
> the cheering* CROWD *surges out through the gates.
> The* KID *rides on their shoulders: immobile in his
> white robe, with one gloved hand extended, the
> golden belt draped around his neck and a towel
> over his head—his smashed and reddened face is
> barely visible—*HE *resembles the lifelike wooden
> saints in Catholic processions. Joyfully his bearers
> parade him before the audience, and with a final
> cheer fling their straw hats into the air*)

CURTAIN

ABOUT THE AUTHOR

HOWARD SACKLER is well experienced as a director as well as a playwright. He is the winner of the 1954 Maxwell Anderson Award and Chicago's Sergel Award. He has received grants from the Rockefeller and Littauer foundations. His new play, *The Pastime of Monsieur Robert*, is scheduled for production by the American Conservatory Theatre.

AESCHYLUS & CO.

BANTAM BESTSELLERS

OUTSTANDING BOOKS NOW AVAILABLE
AT A FRACTION
OF THEIR ORIGINAL COST!